Punctuation at Work

•────────────────────────────────•

Simple Principles for Achieving Clarity
and Good Style

RICHARD LAUCHMAN

⁄AMACOM

AMERICAN MANAGEMENT ASSOCIATION
New York • Atlanta • Brussels • Chicago • Mexico City • San Francisco
Shanghai • Tokyo • Toronto • Washington, D.C.

Bulk discounts available. For details visit:
www.amacombooks.org/go/specialsales
Or contact special sales:
Phone: 800-250-5308
Email: specialsls@amanet.org
View all the AMACOM titles at: www.amacombooks.org

Library of Congress Cataloging-in-Publication Data

Lauchman, Richard.
  Punctuation at work : simple principles for achieving clarity and good style / Richard Lauchman.
        p. cm.
  Includes index.
  ISBN-13: 978-0-8144-1494-1 (pbk.)
  ISBN-10: 0-8144-1494-X (pbk.)
  1. English language–Punctuation. I. American Management Association. II. Title.
  PE1450.L36 2010
  428.2—dc22

                                    2009037753

About AMA

American Management Association (www.amanet.org) is a world leader in talent development, advancing the skills of individuals to drive business success. Our mission is to support the goals of individuals and organizations through a complete range of products and services, including classroom and virtual seminars, webcasts, webinars, podcasts, conferences, corporate and government solutions, business books, and research. AMA's approach to improving performance combines experiential learning—learning through doing—with opportunities for ongoing professional growth at every step of one's career journey.

Printing Number

10   9   8   7   6   5   4   3   2   1

For my daughter, Mackenzie.
Apparuit iam beatitudo vestra.

—Dante, *La Vita Nuova*

Contents

Introduction

This book is for those of you who have to write at work and want clear, commonsense guidance on punctuation. It concerns the usages that are simple, useful, and appropriate in workplace writing, where the chief goal of any document is to convey information as efficiently as possible. Other sorts of writing may seek to enthrall, beguile, amuse, or contribute to the body of human knowledge. But busy executives are not hoping to be enraptured or moved to giggles by an audit report. They want to know, right away, whether they need to take action. And one reason why corporate policies aren't written in Shakespearean verse is that readers of policies are neither seeking nor expecting a literary experience. They simply want to know, in the clearest language possible, what their rights and responsibilities are.

Certainly, in the writing we do at work, our readers deserve this "clearest language possible." I think it's healthy to take pride in your writing, and sensible to care about it, but wise to realize that the main aim of style in workplace writing is to make things easy for the reader. I'm going to show you how punctuation can contribute to simplicity of style. In practical terms, the marks are nothing more than tools for tightening the nuts and bolts of the airy stuff we call meaning. They're as unglamorous and mundane as any collection of wrenches and screwdrivers—and once we get rid of the stupefying half-truths and fallacies about them, they're just as easy to use.

Why So Many Professionals Are Befuddled by Punctuation

No one is born with a sense of where to put a comma. The kitten knows how to pounce, but the child lacks instinct for hyphenating his compound adjectives. We all have to learn how to punctuate, and that means we're at the mercy of those who teach us.

After a quarter-century of teaching writing in the workplace, I'm no longer surprised by the sloppy and confusing punctuation I see in most business, technical, scientific, and regulatory writing. What still surprises me is the number of people who insist that they never received any instruction in the matter. They do not say they never got any "good" instruction or any "reasonable" instruction; they do not say they were confused to the point of paralysis by inconsistencies in what they were taught. What they say is that they were never taught how to use the marks. And the frequency of this complaint is increasing. In the United States it is possible these days to proceed through high school, college, and graduate school with one's instructors encouraging the joys of expression and assuming that teaching clarity of expression is someone else's responsibility.

This is not to say that punctuation is never taught along the way, because it usually is—in ways that make a practical man's hair stand on end. Often, instructors explain only a few crude and elementary usages, leaving unexplored the numerous options essential to a good writer. (I may be expert at wielding a sledgehammer, but if that's the only tool I know how to use, what do I do when I have to extract a splinter?) The guidance writers receive from one year to the next can be slapdash and whimsical, governed by the individual instructor's personal preference, taste, and overall feel for what constitutes good writing. From one year to the next, this guidance can be conflicting and even contradictory. As a freshman one may learn that using parentheses is practically an immoral act; as a sophomore that parentheses are useful, but that dashes are villainous; and as a junior that dashes are the cat's meow, but that semicolons are the footprints of a chuckle-head, or at least evidence of careless thinking.

It should come as no surprise that some instructors, ham-handed or not, simply do not know the conventions of meaning and form. Others may be unaware of important distinctions of usage. Such instructors, often with great force, insist that *however* must always be followed by a comma, that *which* must always be preceded by a comma, that items in any bulleted list must be followed by semicolons, and so on. There are plenty of English teachers and composition instructors who are either mistaken about certain conventions or who were taught the British conventions. In either case, what they plant in fertile and impressionable young minds are the seeds of confusion and error.

And then we have those who learned correct usage decades and decades ago, when (for example) *cooperate* required a hyphen, and it was considered the pinnacle of good taste to introduce abbreviations with great formality, as in *American Telephone and Telegraph Corporation (hereinafter referred to as "AT&T")*. Usage has changed since then. We have all been annoyed by the weather reporter on the radio who tells us there is a zero chance of rain while we have the windshield wipers on maximum. That reporter is reading from a script, not looking through the window to see what's really going on. And instructors who do not bother to read well-written current stuff—to read it with their eyes open, noticing how the marks are truly used—continue to report from the 1960s and to insist that archaic conventions remain in force.

To this bubbling stew of misguidance, we add the two absurd methods of instruction that have victimized writers for decades. The first of these methods is what I call the "sound-bite" method. An example is the famous "Put in a comma where you'd take a breath." The second is one we might call the "I-can't-explain-it-simply-so-I'm-going-to-use-jargon" method. An example of this one is the terrifying and ultimately meaningless rule "A non-restrictive appositive used as a summative modifier is set off with a comma." Ninety-nine percent of the people I work with day in and day out do not remember the jargon of grammar, if indeed they were ever exposed to it. Is it any mystery why people need help with punctuation?

It seems to me there is a middle ground between the breezy impressionism of the sound-biters and the religious jargon chanted by English teachers, Freshman Composition instructors, and others (including managers in the workplace) who cannot fathom the expressions of perplexity, despair, and infinite boredom on the faces of their victims. I have attempted to occupy that middle ground here. Avoiding the sound-bite approach means using a few more words to explain the matter; refusing to use jargon also has the inevitable effect of increasing length. Assuming that you want the complete picture, and not a fragment of it, and assuming you would like to read clear thought in plain English, I take my time and use as many words as my meaning requires.

I intend to show you, explaining as necessary along the way, not only how to use the marks correctly, but how to choose the marks that best clarify your intention and best suggest how much emphasis you want to place on an idea. You'll probably have to throw out (or at least reconsider) some advice you've accepted as rule, but you'll come away with a complete understanding of the "final polish" that good punctuation provides to your structures of thought.

This book explains punctuation in the way I wish it had been explained to me: patiently, thoroughly, systematically, and in words I understand. You will not encounter such terms as "adverbial participle" or "interruptive infinitive" here; and when I refer to a sentence, I call it a sentence, and not, in the new fashion that pretends to be more precise, a "clause complex." There is no need to make the matter more complicated than it is. What I do need to do is overcome the wild guidance you've received over the years and replace it with sensible advice.

Of Ugly Semicolons and Hideous Hoes

I'm a practical man. If I have a hammer and a monkey wrench and I need to tighten a bolt, I'll use the monkey wrench. And I won't spout a lot of philosophy while I do. I just want to get the job done as efficiently as I can.

With my hammer and wrench, I'm able to perform a number of tasks quite well—but if I have only those tools and need to remove a screw, I'll make a great mess of things. If I had a screwdriver, I could get the job done in a flash. It's the same with punctuation. Each of the marks has functions it is best suited to perform. We should know what those functions are and use whichever mark best accomplishes the job at hand. But to use a mark, we must first feel comfortable using it. And if I believe, because someone once told me so, that parentheses are signs of laziness and that semicolons indicate a careless mind, what am I going to do when clarity requires parentheses instead of commas, or when emphasis calls for a semicolon rather than a period?

Now if someone said to you, "Pliers are never necessary" or "Hoes are hideous," you'd probably assume the speaker was either kidding or mentally ill. You'd assume this because your experience has taught you that pliers are often useful—and you might, with good reason, wonder what anyone could find hideous about a hoe. But what if a person of great renown and authority were to make such an asinine statement? When that happens, many people accept the remark as gospel, simply because it comes from the hero. "Spoons are for weaklings," says the hero, and instantly the congregation begins eating porridge with forks. And here we have Winston Churchill saying, "One must regard the hyphen as a blemish to be avoided wherever possible." We have the novelist Donald Barthelme remarking, "The semicolon is ugly, ugly as a tick on a dog's belly." What was that about the hideous hoe?

You don't have to be famous or formally published to voice your opinions as fact. On a casual stroll through the bustling bazaar of the World Wide Web, we encounter dozens of hucksters hawking their aesthetic preferences as revealed truth. "Use parentheses sparingly," says one website devoted to better writing. "Like dashes, they make a page ugly and give the impression of carelessness. If something is worth mentioning, it deserves a sentence of its own."[1] So now parentheses have been indicted as "ugly," and dashes apparently are too. We must put both marks onto the pile with Churchill's hyphen and Barthelme's semicolon. It's probably best not to use them, since they make our pages ugly. "Question marks are just ugly," says another possible expert.[2] "Remember," says another, "slashes are ugly, so use them sparingly."[3] No mark escapes indictment on charges of ugliness and criminal mischief. Meandering online, you find people howling that they are disgusted by commas, sickened by hyphens, nauseated by apostrophes, and revolted by brackets, quotation marks, and exclamation points.

Yes, on the Web it is child's play to find overexcited remarks about anything under the sun. But the sentiments quoted here are hardly exceptional. And they demonstrate nothing we don't already know: that many people are thoroughly frustrated by punctuation, and that what people actually say about the marks can be so utterly impressionistic and overgeneralized as to verge on the insane. It is ludicrous to hate the wrench and preposterous to call it ugly.

Where the Advice in This Book Comes From

The way we use punctuation is governed by convention. Everyone agrees that we end a declarative sentence with a period, use quotation marks to indicate we're citing exact words, and so on. Where there are disputes about usage, these disputes are not terribly harmful to clarity. How much difference does it make, really, that the *New York Times* prefers *I.B.M.* (with periods) and the *Washington Post* prefers *IBM* (without them)? Is it truly a cause for concern that the *Times* prefers *Davis' house* (adding only the apostrophe to make *Davis* possessive) and the *Post* considers *Davis's house* to be better?

The usages presented here show punctuation as it is practiced in the United States by newspapers and magazines that have a wide readership. We must take our standards from somewhere, and it seems to me that periodicals such as *Science, Newsweek*, and *National Geographic* do more than simply communicate well to people of all levels of education—they also confirm and reinforce what punctuation conventions are. By reading these periodicals (and the *Dallas Morning News*, the *Boston Globe*, the *Wall Street Journal*, and so forth), we unconsciously acquire a sense of how punctuation contributes to meaning. Without thinking about it, we recognize the distinction between *When do we eat, Mom?* and *When do we eat Mom?*

Where there is disagreement about usage, I take the side of the reader and—possibly boldly—recommend that we neither insult her intelligence nor complicate her getting what we mean. I believe that in terms of handling the mechanics of the language, it's best to be conservative: to honor convention where convention holds, and where there is disagreement, to select the option that most economically conveys our intent.

How to Get the Most out of This Book

Start by reading "Definitions." That short section explains the few terms necessary to simplify the discussion. We cannot make much headway if we don't agree on what "intention" means, and knowing what a dependent clause is takes the guesswork out of punctuating some very common constructions. I encourage you to read that section, and for two reasons. First, people use different terms to refer to the same concept: for example, "non-essential language," "non-restrictive expression," and "parenthetical expression" all denote stuff you could cut from the sentence. Second, I am going to use particular definitions precisely and consistently when discussing how to use the marks.

Next, read "What You Need to Know First." Here you'll find 19 short essays that, together, provide the conceptual framework that skilled writers use intuitively when they punctuate. Read them, and you'll know what you're doing when you choose a mark, rather than hoping that the choice makes something clear. You'll also come away with much more flexibility in suggesting subtle shades of meaning. This section explains, one principle at a time, what you need to know before you decide whether and how to punctuate a structure of language. It also digs underneath the surface of "rules" and shows you how and why the marks signal certain nuances of emphasis. (This is useful to know when you have alternative ways of punctuating an expression.) Finally, it addresses several important issues in punctuation that require more than a paragraph to explain. This stuff is essential to understand, and no one ever bothers to explain it. I put it in a separate section so that I don't need to repeat it over and over.

In "The Marks," all of the marks are listed alphabetically, beginning with the apostrophe and ending with the slash. For each mark, every use pertinent to workplace writing is covered, and each usage is illustrated by several business-related examples. But the guidance will make much more sense if you read the two preliminary sections first.

The last section, "Punctuating Common Sentence Structures," shows exactly how the marks work in the heat of battle. It mirrors the guidance from the previous section, but its focus is on the language structure itself, not on the many uses of the individual marks. The repetition is intentional: I know from experience in the classroom that certain concepts require reiteration, and this is especially true when we first have to scrape off the thick crust of half-truths and generalizations you've picked up over the years.

Author's Note

Anyone who writes about punctuation brings his own preferences to the matter. But there are two kinds of preferences—those that complicate understanding, and those that simplify it. I have some; I admit it. But I refer to them as "preferences" and not as "prejudices," because a preference may have some reason behind it, while a prejudice does not. And ultimately, regardless of what we call them, we need to examine their validity not from the point of view of the writer, but from the point of view that matters: the reader's. A number of "correct" usages can actually interfere with clarity, and we should avoid them. When we have options, we should select the one that simplifies understanding, not the one that proves we know the rules.

When I can't find a way to bypass the matter, I use *he* and *she* interchangeably throughout. To me this practice is less distracting than using *he or she, his/her*, and *s/he*.

From the examples provided you'll see that this book focuses on workplace writing: memos, correspondence, reports, analyses, policies, presentations, and all the other stuff that people have to write on the job. But—and this is important—the guidance in this book applies to any kind of writing where clarity is the chief goal.[1]

Definitions

Clause: An expression that contains a subject and a verb. There are two kinds of clauses, and here's what they look like:

Independent clauses	*Dependent clauses*
I see	unless I see
they discussed the contract	after they discussed the contract
the printer is malfunctioning	if the printer is malfunctioning

Dependent clause: A clause that begins with a word like *when, because, after, before, until, unless, since, although, whenever,* or *if.* The dependent clause isn't a full-fledged sentence. It's called "dependent" because its sense depends on how it's attached to an independent clause. Here are a few more examples of dependent clauses:

whenever I try to read her writing	because his brain was damaged
until we document the problem	after we receive your proposal
before he joined the company	though we have heard nothing from them

Independent clause: The basic sentence. It's called "independent" because it can stand alone. Independent clauses look like this:

We interviewed 50 applicants.	The species is thriving.
These molecules are unstable.	When will you send the contract?
She finally faced the truth.	Answer the phone!

Clear: Let's use a practical definition. When the reader instantly gets your intended meaning, your sentence is clear. By that definition, if he has to read the sentence twice to get your intention, it isn't clear, but at least it manages to convey your thought. If the reader has to study the sentence for a time and remains unsure of what you mean, it's unclear.

If you write a sentence that logically expresses an idea you don't intend, it makes no sense to refer to that sentence as "clear," regardless of how perfectly it conforms to the conventions of the language, and regardless of whether the reader manages to guess correctly at your meaning.

Romanov's novel *Shiny* won the National Book Award.

Romanov's novel, *Shiny*, won the National Book Award.

Each of those sentences expresses a clear meaning, but the meanings differ. If you intend to indicate that Romanov has written only one novel, then the second version is what you must write. Given what you intend to convey, we'd say that the first one isn't clear, even though it does clearly express a thought.

One more example:

As her sources of inspiration, Ms. Growlie mentioned her two sisters, Mother Teresa and Joan of Arc.

As her sources of inspiration, Ms. Growlie mentioned her two sisters, Mother Teresa, and Joan of Arc.

Each of those expresses a clear thought as well. But the first one implies that Mother Teresa and Joan of Arc are Ms. Growlie's sisters—and if you mean that Ms. Growlie mentioned four sources of inspiration, then you must write the second one. Again, using our definition of clarity, we would have to say that the first one fails the test of being clear.

Conjunction: A word used to connect ideas. There are several distinct groups of conjunctions, and of course each group has a scary name.

Coordinating conjunction: *and, but, or, so, nor, for, yet,* and *as* are the coordinating conjunctions in English. We use them to connect words (*precise* and *thorough*), phrases (*from IBM* or *from Hewlett-Packard*), and clauses (*Resistance is futile,* but *you can still complain*).

Conjunctive adverb: *however, therefore, moreover, otherwise,* and *nevertheless* are examples of the many conjunctive adverbs. They serve as transitions between independent clauses. Don't concern yourself with why they're called adverbs; all you need to do is know how to punctuate one when you use it.

Correlative conjunction: *either/or, neither/nor,* and *not only/but also* are the most common correlative conjunctions. They come in pairs and they serve to set up either comparison or contrast.

Subordinating conjunction: *because, when, if, unless,* and *although* are examples. There are dozens of them in English, and they're used to begin clauses. The only thing you need to know is that when you begin a clause with one of these words, that clause is dependent and can't stand alone.

Convention: What a group (in this case, speakers of English) decides is the normal or standard way of doing something. It's conventional, for example, to begin a sentence with a capital letter, use *I* (not *O*) for the first-person pronoun, and form possessives with *'s*. Convention determines how we engineer meaning in all aspects of language. And it's from convention that we derive ideas of what's correct and incorrect.

Correct: I'm going to set a high standard for "correctness." We are not going to use the English teacher's abstract definition that requires only correctness of form. If we evaluate form alone, the following sentence is correct:

> The annual AARP membership fee is $10, which includes a spouse at no extra charge.

There's nothing wrong with form: nothing is misspelled, grammar is perfect, and punctuation is fine. The only thing wrong with the sentence is that it says something, perfectly clearly, that the writer does not mean: that for 10 bucks you get a spouse. For our purposes, that sentence is "incorrect"—and this is because our purposes are practical (not abstract, academic, or philosophical).

In the practical world, you must not be satisfied with any sentence until it meets this definition of correctness: the sentence both conforms to the standards and, according to the conventions of meaning, embodies your intent. (I use "embodies" instead of "conveys" because whether the reader grasps the intent is beyond your control.)

> The task force is searching for the F-117 lost over the Red Sea.

> The task force is searching for the F-117, lost over the Red Sea.

Both of those are correct *in form*, but the first expression indicates that more than one F-117 is missing; the second indicates that only one F-117 is missing. In this case, if you intend the first thought but write the second expression, the sentence fails the test of correctness. I realize that this is a rugged standard, but it's the one that counts.

Emphatic: Describes an expression that nails the writer's intended emphasis. Only the writer knows what she wishes to emphasize and how much emphasis each idea deserves. Some structures of language could be punctuated in several different ways, and the alternative we choose should indicate the nuance we intend. Thus, while all three of the examples below are clear and correct *in form*, only one of them can be emphatic. If I want you to regard *though he may have been joking* as a very minor point, my intent requires parentheses.

> He said, though he may have been joking, that the idea struck him while he was stuck in traffic.

> He said (though he may have been joking) that the idea struck him while he was stuck in traffic.

> He said—though he may have been joking—that the idea struck him while he was stuck in traffic.

Intention: What you want your expression to mean to your reader. I'm going to use "intended meaning," "intention, and "intent" interchangeably.

Mishandled punctuation often twists or conceals the writer's intention. In the examples below, assume that the writer intends the meaning of the second expression. In each case, the words are in the right order, but the meaning is hidden.

Richard needs to be careful:	She is dressed to kill Richard.
Richard is being addressed:	She is dressed to kill, Richard.
Severnius is described (and probably displeased):	Members of the panel include Professor Severnius, a vampire fetishist and a convicted embezzler.
Severnius is now one of three:	Members of the panel include Professor Severnius, a vampire fetishist, and a convicted embezzler.
The intention is puzzling:	Change each issue to matter.
The intention is made plain:	Change each "issue" to "matter."

List: A series of ideas. The most common lists consist of nouns, verbs, adverbs, or adjectives. Here's what simple lists look like:

nouns	They have offices in New York, Chicago, Los Angeles, and Dallas.
verbs	We collected, tested, analyzed, and classified the water samples.
adverbs	She handled the problem quickly, thoroughly, and professionally.
adjectives	We commend her for her quick, thorough, and professional response.

You can list anything—full sentences, clauses, phrases, citations, equations, you name it. The many shapes of lists are punctuated in differing ways. For a thorough discussion of lists, see the appendix, "How to List Ideas."

Parenthetical expression: An expression you could cut from the sentence without damaging your primary intent. It's called "parenthetical" because it merely adds a little qualifying information or description. (The term comes directly from the Greek *parenthesis*, which means literally "putting in beside.") Here are a few examples, with the parenthetical expressions in italics. Note that these expressions are always punctuated.

Eli Yingling *(the company's former chief of security)* has agreed to testify.

The central bank lowered its federal funds rate—*the rate it charges banks for overnight loans*—by three-quarters of a percentage point.

The CFO, *aghast at the expense*, quickly ended the policy.

Parenthetical expressions sometimes appear at the beginning and ending of sentences.

According to witnesses, the postman bit the dog.

> She had divorced for the fifth time when she wrote her first book, *The Joys of Nagging*.

To keep matters simple (and because it does no harm whatsoever), I'm going to call the italicized stuff below "parenthetical" too.

> *Glaring at the judge*, the defense attorney closed his mouth and sat down.

> Five crows sat on the telephone wires, *looking like notes on a sheet of music*.

Purists of grammar would differ with me on what to call those expressions, but that's okay. The practical point is that the phrases could be removed from the sentences without damaging the primary intent. All you need to do is recognize that, and you'll understand that you need to punctuate them.

Primary intent: The main idea of the sentence; the main thought you want to convey. This is a grammatical consideration that comes into play only when you begin adding non-essential words. In *He was terrified of his third-grade teacher*, every word is essential to meaning. The primary intent is the same in *He was terrified of his third-grade teacher, Sister Beatrice*. The phrase *Sister Beatrice* serves merely to name the teacher. Because it could be removed from the sentence without affecting the primary meaning, it must be punctuated.

Punctuation: (1) A bunch of impossible-to-figure-out marks, invented by the devil to give writers a foretaste of hell, taught in a hundred confusing and contradictory ways. (2) A code, used in writing, that is often necessary for meaning and for emphasis. The code originated in attempts to capture, in text, the various stops, pauses, and inflections of speech. Today it is logical in application. Both writers and readers need to understand it and pay attention to it.

Reader: A person whose job is to apply his intellect to what's written on the page in an honest attempt to understand the writer's intention.

He is not responsible for reading the writer's mind; his responsibility begins and ends with reading what the writer has actually put on the page. When he lacks a sufficient grasp of how language engineers meaning, then it doesn't matter how well the text is written.

Restrictive and non-restrictive expressions: A restrictive expression limits meaning. If I have more than one brother, I write *My brother Paul lives in Scotland*. The word *Paul* restricts the meaning of *brother* by specifying the brother I'm talking about. *Paul* is not parenthetical; it's necessary to my meaning and it isn't punctuated.

On the other hand, if I have only one brother, I write *My brother, Paul, lives in Scotland*. In this case, because I have only one brother, the word *Paul* doesn't serve to identify a particular brother but only to tell you what my brother's name is. In this case, *Paul* is parenthetical, or *non-restrictive*. The word could be removed from the sentence, and to show you that, I put commas around it. The sentence is correct *in form* with or without commas; punctuation here is a matter of being accurate in what you imply.

Writer: A person whose duty is to be clear. This is a moral and ethical obligation, and every decision (from word choice to format) must spring from it. When a writer lacks a sufficient grasp of how language engineers meaning, then her ethics, however virtuous they may be, are irrelevant.

"You moron!" (1) What a reader shouts at a writer who, for any of a number of reasons, has failed to make his meaning plain. (2) What a writer shouts at a reader who, for any number of reasons, has misunderstood a structure of language that would instantly be clear to everyone else. (3) What both writer and reader shout at one another when each party believes his point of view is justified and the other's is ridiculous.

To avoid the circumstances that provoke this shout, both writer and reader must satisfy two conditions. First, they must agree on how structures of language create meaning and suggest emphasis—for example, they must agree that *employee's rights* and *employees' rights* have different meanings and they must agree on what those meanings are. They must also agree that *vegetarian octogenarian* emphasizes one's age, while *octogenarian vegetarian* emphasizes one's diet. In other words, they have to share a sense of the conventions of the language. Second, they must cooperate. The writer must do his utmost to make his meaning plain to the readers he's actually addressing. The reader must approach the text in good faith, with the assumption that the writer is doing his utmost to convey an idea, that every word on the page is there for a reason, and that nothing important has been left out.

Yunder: The place where pure and perfect meaning resides. It's just down the street from Valhalla.

In the practical world, the chief weakness of meaning is that it exists only in an isolated and imperfect human mind. Thus it is always a private matter and is always somewhat dented, rumpled, and wrinkled by the particular inflections of that mind. The onerous reality is that human minds are not merely incapable of telepathy, but are fallible in other ways: prone to error, hasty in judgment, sometimes deceptive, eager to argue, keen on showing off, fond of rationalizing, and quick to blame others. This is what accounts for the incessant cries of "You moron!" in every workplace.

But in the bright halls of Yunder, meaning floats free and pure, unadulterated by incarceration in a human intellect. When a writer is certain she has made her meaning plain, she believes she has snatched her expression straight from Yunder. When a reader struggles to understand a writer's intent and rephrases it until he finally grasps it, he bitterly assumes that his rephrasing is certainly verbatim from Yunder. It's a pity that no earthly visa can gain us entrance there. Even a brief visit would settle a lot of arguments.

What You Need to Know First: 19 Principles

1. Punctuation can't rescue sense from nonsense.

Before you punctuate, make sure you've used the right words and have put those words in a sensible order. If you haven't, the marks won't help. Punctuation is perfect in the sentences below, but the writer isn't saying what he means.

> As a 6-year-old girl, my grandfather owned a 40-acre farm.

> I always feed my dog before I eat myself.

> In her affidavit, the plaintiff contends she was insulted on several occasions by the elevator.

> All of these details are not relevant.

> Etymology often fails to elucidate contemporary lexical utility.

The first sentence states flatly that the grandfather was once a 6-year-old girl. From the second, we can only wonder what the dog gets to eat. The third sentence can easily be read to mean that the elevator lacks manners. The fourth is ambiguous. How many of the details are irrelevant? All of them, or only some of them? And the last one illustrates what happens when we try to sound "profound": difficult words obstruct meaning. Such writing might charm professors reviewing a doctoral dissertation in linguistics, but in the workplace our readers deserve better. We are pursuing instant clarity, and the best way to achieve it is to state the idea plainly: *A word's origin often has nothing to do with how the word is used today.*

Punctuation is not a magic wand we can wave at lumps of language to bring them to life and declare a clear meaning. The most gifted punctuator on the planet can't yank sense from a construction if the words are mutinous in the first place. Whether punctuation is handled well or poorly is beside the point in long, ramshackle sentences like the ones below. Debating how best to punctuate such sentences is like debating what shade of lipstick would most beautify a chimp.

> The undersigned has devised a narrative that delineates the chronological aspects of a given environment, twice pronounced in different configurations, of which one is decidedly superior to its counterpart.

> Recent investigations which have indicated that pharmacologic stimulation of alveolization is possible in both neonatal mice and in a mature mouse model of emphysema have also been corroborated in a lamb model of prematurity.

> We anticipate that the results of this project will provide the DoD researchers with a software package that will provide polycrystalline material modelers access to accurate 3D digital microstructure models that are validated by direct comparison to experimental recrystallization data and an automated microstructure and grid generation process to produce the FE mesh for the complex microstructure systems.

See punctuation as a "final polish."

Understand the limits of what punctuation can accomplish. *Do first things first.* Confine your choice of words to those your reader understands; within that limit, choose the most precise words; put those words in meaningful order; keep your sentences to a manageable length. Only after you do these things can punctuation make a difference.

2. The main reason to punctuate is to clarify your intent.

In English, it's all too easy to mislead the reader. The synonym-heavy language enables us to misbehave and write *Your execution is requested* when we mean *Please sign it*. Unaccompanied by a photograph, the headline *American Ships Head to Gibraltar* strikes some readers as particularly macabre—at least until they read the lead sentence and realize that the story is about the U.S. Navy, and not about someone's shipping his head overseas. The same words, in the same order, can suggest one thing to Susan and another thing to Sam. And because this is so, we are always in danger of writing something ambiguous or, worse, something that conveys a clear meaning we do not intend.

Every sentence has two kinds of meaning.

In the practical world, when we talk about the meaning of a sentence, we're referring to the writer's intent. When we ask, "What does this mean?" we're really asking something on the order of "What do you want me to understand?" or "What are you trying to say?"

Sometimes we ask this because of various confusing faults in the writing—a modifier put where it could refer to two things, a pronoun with a vague reference, crippled parallelism, and so on. But even the grammatically perfect sentence has two kinds of meaning: the writer's intended meaning, and a brutish, abstract, "plausible" meaning made logically possible by the way language works. The two should be identical, but sometimes they don't quite match.

> Several hundred prostitutes are appealing to the Pope.

When I write that sentence, my intended meaning is that the prostitutes are taking their grievance to the Pope. It does say that, and most readers will understand it that way. But I shouldn't be surprised if some sly readers snicker at the idea that the Pope finds several hundred prostitutes appealing. It says that too—or at least it can be construed to say that, according to how the language engineers meaning.

Let's assume that context and common sense come to the rescue here, and that readers who chuckle at the second meaning also understand it isn't the intended one. And because the reader's common sense would ultimately discard the second interpretation, I wouldn't call the sentence "ambiguous." I'd call it an amusing slip worth remembering, but it isn't ambiguous to a reader with experience of the world.

> Several hundred prostitutes are asking the Pope to intervene.

> Several hundred prostitutes are appealing the decision
> to the Pope.

> Several hundred prostitutes are taking their grievance
> to the Pope.

If I write the thought in one of those ways, the two kinds of meaning overlay one another. Simply put, only my intent is expressed. Only my intent is plausible; no other meaning can reasonably be construed.

Syntax (the order of words) is often enough to create and convey the sense we intend. *I read the report this morning* requires only a period at the end, as does *The attorney left her briefcase in the cab*. But even if we wrote nothing but short declarative sentences, we would still occasionally need help in clarifying our intention. When syntax alone fails to make meaning plain, punctuation shows the sense you want your words to make. There is a decided difference in meaning between *the little-used car* and *the little, used car*.

And this is the chief reason for punctuating: to clarify the intent of a structure of language that would—or simply might—otherwise be confusing or misleading. If I intend to state what first responders must do, I write *First responders must secure the area*; but if I intend to state what any responders must do first, I write *First, responders must secure the area*. The words are in the right order, and punctuation clarifies my intent. If I intend to tell you my impression of someone's words, I write *The words he used were disgusting and obscene*, but if I intend to tell you what words he used, I write *The words he used were "disgusting" and "obscene."*

Use whichever marks are necessary to make your intention plain.

I'm mentioning this only because some of you have been taught, by those who confuse personal preference with convention, that dashes are inappropriate in workplace writing, that parentheses should be used only to introduce abbreviations, that certain constructions never require a hyphen, and so on. Operating under such restrictions is tantamount to shooting yourself in the knee and then wondering why you can't jog. Writers are entitled to as many biases as they like, but not at the reader's expense; the writer's right to prejudice about punctuation stops when a prejudice interferes with clarity. As you read through these principles, you'll see that every mark in the arsenal is necessary, at one time or another, for clarifying not merely your meaning but also your intended emphasis.

3. One of punctuation's tasks is to supply the various signals given by the voice.

In conveying intention, speakers have a great advantage over writers. The speaker's audience can hear the many stops, pauses, and nuances of tone provided by the voice. The writer's audience must rely on text— and text is silent. Punctuation suggests how your voice would behave if you were speaking.

> Marie Antoinette embraced him warmly half an hour after her head was cut off.

If that thought strikes you as bizarre, it's only because you do not hear the writer's voice. Here's the same order of words, punctuated to indicate where (and for how long) the writer would pause to show the separation of ideas:

> Marie Antoinette embraced him warmly. Half an hour after, her head was cut off.

Punctuation originated for precisely this reason—to show, in text, the various stops, pauses, and inflections of the speaker. The word comes from the Latin *punctus* ("sharp point"), which is what the Romans called the little mark they used to indicate a major break in thought. Today we call that mark a "period."

> The prosecutor was found in contempt of court because he ignored the judge's repeated warnings he was sentenced to 10 days in jail.

A listener could easily hear how a speaker intends that expression to be understood. The reader can't. The writer uses punctuation to show how his voice would demonstrate his intent:

> The prosecutor was found in contempt of court. Because he ignored the judge's repeated warnings, he was sentenced to 10 days in jail.

or

> The prosecutor was found in contempt of court because he ignored the judge's repeated warnings. He was sentenced to 10 days in jail.

You might ask Benedict to pass the eggs, or Béarnaise to pass the sauce. When you address someone by name, you naturally pause an instant first. On the page, the comma indicates this natural pause.

> Please pass the eggs, Benedict.

> Please pass the sauce, Béarnaise.

Writing must reflect such pauses, because you would be asking for something else entirely if you omitted the comma:

> Please pass the eggs Benedict.

> Please pass the sauce Béarnaise.

These distinctions in meaning are conventional—but convention, like a dog, needs an occasional walk in the fresh air. If context makes clear that there is no eggs Benedict on the table, that some other form of eggs is on the table, and that Benedict is one of the diners, then readers understand that *Please pass the eggs Benedict* is a request addressed to Benedict. They do. They get it. The comma simply helps them get it a little more quickly.

I said earlier that text is silent. Let me now qualify that. Text is silent in the way sheet music is silent: one who can read music notation can easily imagine—in effect, can "hear"—the notes, the tempo, and the volume. Punctuation provides such signals too.

We aren't talking about meaning anymore; now we're talking about emphasis.

> This action would certainly bankrupt the company.

> This action would, certainly, bankrupt the company.

Both of those are correct and clear, but they differ subtly in emphasis. In the second expression, the commas around *certainly* stress the word because they segregate it. They suggest that the speaker would pause slightly, before and after the word, in order to make sure you hear its cargo. I want to stress that I am *not* saying "use a comma where you'd pause" and leaving it at that. The adage applies only to emphasis, never to clarity (which is governed by rule). In matters of emphasis, punctuation is sometimes discretionary, and good judgment is essential.[1]

Punctuation takes the place of the voice not merely in matters of pausing and stopping (to separate ideas), but also in matters of inflection. When we speak, we change pace, pitch, tone, and volume to emphasize and de-emphasize ideas. Below, note how punctuation can characterize the same event in three different ways.

> The district attorney said, tongue in cheek, that he didn't give a fig about First Amendment rights.

> The district attorney said (tongue in cheek) that he didn't give a fig about First Amendment rights.

The district attorney said—tongue in cheek—that he didn't give a fig about First Amendment rights.

For reasons I'll address later, punctuation is required around "tongue in cheek." What's important now is that there are three ways to punctuate the phrase. Each supplies a different signal about what you would hear if you were listening to the writer *speak* the sentence. The commas indicate only mild pauses for logical separation; the speaker's voice would neither rise nor drop. Parentheses suggest the voice would drop, which would be the speaker's way of letting us know that "tongue in cheek" is a minor idea, just barely worth mentioning. Dashes, on the other hand, suggest that the speaker would pause a little longer before and after the phrase, and possibly raise his voice a bit, to make sure we hear that the attorney didn't actually mean what he said.[2]

It's important to keep in mind that while punctuation originated to indicate the stops and pauses of speech, its application is now governed by logic. Another way of putting it is that we now have a series of conventions—in many cases, a system of rules—that form the code for making something mean what it means. The physics of convention, not the behavior of the voice, is why there's a difference in meaning between *I read it too, casually* and *I read it too casually*.

4. In workplace writing, a sentence should yield its meaning instantly.

Let's agree that common sense, context, experience of the world, and a grasp of how language works are important to our understanding any structure of language. Let's agree that readers can often (after some effort) tease out the intended meaning of an initially puzzling expression and ultimately understand what the writer is trying to say. But let's also agree that making sense is the writer's responsibility. In the writing we do at work, efficiency counts: we want the reader to understand what we mean the first time he reads the sentence.

This efficiency is a simple courtesy to the reader, whose time isn't wasted by having to read the same sentence twice. In turn, the same courtesy is our best hope of keeping the reader interested in reading our text and focused on what we're trying to convey.

◆ ◆ ◆

When his wife walked in his body was lying face-down.

In that sentence from a police report, common sense suggests—after an instant—that his wife didn't actually walk in his body. Readers end up with the intended meaning. But *When his wife walked in, his body was lying face-down* is what the writer means, conveys the thought simply, does not distract, and thus is what the writer should have written. Here, a comma instantly clarifies intent.

◆ ◆ ◆

For best when used by information, please see the date printed on the package.

That one comes from a candy wrapper. That's its context. But here the reader needs some experience of the world, specifically of the convention known as the "expiration date." And even with this experience, you have to puzzle out the meaning, which could have been made clear with quotation marks: *For "best when used by" information, please see the date printed on the package.*[3]

◆ ◆ ◆

We have received proposals from Corvas, MacLeod and Tanner and Lynch.

That sentence comes from a short report that discusses a number of contractors. In this instance, even a perfect grasp of context and an abundance of common sense do not help us understand what the writer means. In this instance, what's necessary is what we might call specific background knowledge, namely that *MacLeod and Tanner* is the name of a single firm. At a minimum, the writer should use the serial comma[4]: *We have received proposals from Corvas, MacLeod and Tan-*

ner, and Lynch. But it would be better, in this case, to rephrase the thought and punctuate like this: *We have received proposals from three contractors: Corvas, Lynch, and MacLeod and Tanner.*

A practical writer would not hesitate to use the ampersand here and write *MacLeod & Tanner* if that's the way the company presents its name. The ampersand reinforces the idea that *MacLeod and Tanner* is a unit. Some people, wisely or otherwise, object to its use if *MacLeod and Tanner* formally uses *and.*

◆ ◆ ◆

The proclamation was signed by 50 odd scientists.

There, a meaning is crystal clear, but it doesn't do much to bolster confidence in the worth of the proclamation. Wouldn't the proclamation have more credence if those who signed it weren't crackpots? But what we get isn't what the writer means. He means "approximately 50," and that sense requires a hyphen. Punctuation clarifies intent: *The proclamation was signed by 50-odd scientists.*

◆ ◆ ◆

Use mentally challenged individuals instead of morons from now on.

A reader's reaction to that sentence is a perplexed "What?" The meaning is perfectly clear: the writer is telling us to replace one group with another group. (Readers might be forgiven for wondering what possible difference such a substitution could make.) The problem, again, is that the meaning we get isn't the meaning the writer wants us to get. Here, the right words are in the right order, so quotation marks reveal the intent: *Use "mentally challenged individuals" instead of "morons" from now on.* The writer is not talking about people, but about *terms.*

◆ ◆ ◆

The legislation is bitterly opposed by area farmers and ranchers, who fear that the introduction of wolves into the park would threaten their livestock.

And now we come to the dilemma posed by our readers' varying skill in decoding structures of language. Some readers are more skillful than others. The previous example is beautifully crafted: clear, concise, and correct in every way. And what I am telling readers to get from it is that *all* farmers and ranchers in the area are opposing the legislation.

> The legislation is bitterly opposed by area farmers and ranchers who fear that the introduction of wolves into the park would threaten their livestock.

There's an altogether different meaning. When I do not use a comma after *ranchers*, I am telling readers that only *certain* farmers and ranchers—not all of them, but only the ones who fear for their livestock—are opposing the legislation.[5]

Your reader has some responsibility too.

These distinctions in meaning are what the code of the language supports, but that doesn't make any difference if the reader doesn't know the code. The best we can do as writers is to know how the code works and to craft our meaning according to the conventions of the code. The quarterback's job is to throw the ball in such a way that the receiver has a good chance of catching it. Ultimately, he has no control over whether the receiver catches or drops a well-thrown pass.

5. Punctuation should be invisible.

That's an exaggerated way of saying that readers shouldn't notice the marks you use. We want punctuation to guide and influence the reader, but never to distract him. Ideally, the reader should pay no attention to how we express a thing, and instead simply get whatever ideas we're trying to convey.

Imagine a window. What we want from a window is to look through it and see what's beyond. A clean glass pane does its job by being transparent—we might say it does its job by going unnoticed. But if that pane is dirty, it interferes with our perception of the world. And if it had "Wash me" traced in the grime, or a few yellow sticky notes stuck to it, it would call attention to itself. The surface (the pane) would cease to function as access to the visible world, and would have the status of an object.

It's the same with text. All text consists of two dimensions: the surface (which is made up of a bunch of clamorous symbols on the page) and the thought (which is expressed by that surface but which is ultimately beyond it).

We can call the surface "style." In workplace writing, every aspect of style should be transparent. Nothing should distract the reader; nothing should interfere with his "getting it." Unfortunately, when a writer botches grammar, misspells a word or two, or mangles punctuation, the reader gets distracted and begins looking at the surface of things. She starts searching for additional errors, and she begins asking questions we do not want her to ask, questions such as *Doesn't the writer know better?* or *Didn't the writer bother to proofread?* or *Is it right to use a semicolon after "Dear Mr. Riley"?* Such questions have nothing to do with the point we're trying to make.

We can prevent the reader from asking them by being *conservative* in the way we handle punctuation and every other aspect of style. By "being conservative" here, I mean two things: (1) not making little, distracting errors, and (2) operating within the code your readers expect. Just know the conventions and follow them.

Writers sometimes ignore the conventions we share and instead use a private code. Ultimately, the motives don't matter. What matters is that unusual usages like the ones below call attention to themselves.

> Visitors must park in /designated/ spaces.

> Please send the {executed} contract to the COTR.

> They have agreed --- at long last --- to review our request for reconsideration.

> The committee . . . to our great surprise . . . has decided to terminate funding.

The first two probably indicate a writer's highly personal attempt to emphasize a word; the last two look like devil-may-care attempts to emphasize a phrase. But we don't see such constructions in everyday workplace writing, and because we do not see them, we must pause and ponder them. *Three hyphens? Hmmm. Is that supposed to be more emphatic than a dash? I didn't know we could do that. Is it right? Can I use it too? Should I be using it? And those three dots. Hmmm. Is that supposed to create suspense? Has something been left out? Is the writer trying to suggest he's struggling to find the right words? Hmmm.*

And so, instead of reading, the reader ruminates. Ruminating is excellent if we are cows, but if we are readers we should not be compelled to chew and re-chew. Your punctuation should call no attention to itself.

6. Punctuation follows the arrangement of words.

In English, both meaning and emphasis depend on the order of words.

The dog chased the cat and *The cat chased the dog* consist of exactly the same words, but the different order creates different meanings. Put the words in the right order before you punctuate. When you're the writer, you're the only one who knows what the "right" order is, both for your intended meaning and for emphasis.

The four examples below demonstrate one aspect of emphasis. Note how shifting the grammatical subject (*Redskins, Giants, attorney, contract*) shifts the reader's focus.

in the Washington Post, *emphasizing "Redskins":*	The Redskins beat the Giants.
in the New York Times, *emphasizing "Giants":*	The Giants lost to the Redskins.
emphasizing "attorney":	The attorney is reviewing the contract.
emphasizing "contract":	The contract is being reviewed by the attorney.

Intention dictates the order of words, and the order of words dictates whether to punctuate.

Consider these two sentences:

> Dr. Vesuvio suffered a midlife crisis and bought an Aston Martin.

> Dr. Vesuvio, in the midst of a midlife crisis, bought an Aston Martin.

In the first example, I have structured the thought in such a way that every word in the sentence is necessary for my intended meaning. Another way of putting it is that nothing can be cut from the sentence without damaging my intent. In the second example, I am signaling something quite different. This time, I have arranged the words to let you know that my primary intent is *Dr. Vesuvio bought an Aston Martin*. This time, I want you to understand that *in the midst of a midlife crisis* is parenthetical—that is, it's just an extra bit of information; it's not essential to my primary intent. The phrase could be cut from the sentence, and thus it must be punctuated.

It's important to remember who's in charge. The writer is in charge of figuring out what he wants to say, of deciding how much emphasis to place on any idea, and of engineering the right words into the appropriate order. But once he has structured his order of words, that order of words is in charge of punctuation. In the examples below, note how punctuation changes as the order of words changes.

one subject, two verbs:	The police stormed the building and subdued the terrorists.
two independent clauses:	The police stormed the building, and the terrorists quickly surrendered.
one subject, two verbs, and a non-interruptive phrase:	The police stormed the building and subdued the terrorists without firing a shot.

one subject, two verbs, and an   The police stormed the building and,
interruptive phrase: without firing a shot, subdued the
   terrorists.

Be careful when deciding what to make parenthetical.

Both of the sentences below are correct and clear, but they differ in what they emphasize. Punctuation follows the order of the words.

A consultant from TMI, Janis Gibbons, will conduct the study.

Janis Gibbons, a consultant from TMI, will conduct the study.

In the first example, you are telling the reader that the main thought is *A consultant from TMI will conduct the study.* You are also telling her, *Oh, and by the way, the name of the consultant is Janis Gibbons.* In the second example, you are instructing the reader to understand this: *Janis Gibbons will conduct the study. By the way, she's a consultant from TMI.* Context and common sense should guide you in determining which construction is more appropriate.

When an idea is important, don't arrange the words in a way that signals otherwise.

There's a big distinction between an idea's being important enough to say and its being grammatically essential. When you want an idea to be seen as essential, make sure that the grammar reflects it.

The defense attorney insists that the confession, which was given under duress, is inadmissible.

Given the grammar of English, the order of words in that sentence makes *which was given under duress* a non-essential idea. If the writer's primary intention is to say *The defense attorney insists that the confession is inadmissible*, then the sentence works. On the other hand, if the writer intends the *given under duress* idea to be essential, then he must organize the words so that the idea cannot be cut. Here are two ways to do that:

> The defense attorney insists that the confession was given under duress and is thus inadmissible.

> The defense attorney insists that the confession is inadmissible because it was given under duress.

7. Punctuation indicates how ideas relate.

Punctuation can be correct and flimsy at the same time.

It's correct, for example, to use any of five marks between two independent clauses, but the mark you use should show the reader how those clauses truly relate. First, here are the five marks:

period	The survey revealed a surprising statistic.
	Sixty-eight percent of U.S. citizens believe in creationism.
parentheses	The survey revealed a surprising statistic
	(68 percent of U.S. citizens believe in creationism).
semicolon	The survey revealed a surprising statistic;
	68 percent of U.S. citizens believe in creationism.
dash	The survey revealed a surprising statistic—
	68 percent of U.S. citizens believe in creationism.
colon	The survey revealed a surprising statistic:
	68 percent of U.S. citizens believe in creationism.

Each of those is formally correct, but only the last two show exactly how the second thought relates to the first. In the construction above, the first clause raises a question—"What's the surprising statistic?"—and the second clause instantly answers that question. This construction is called a "summary statement," and when you write one of those, you should use a colon or a dash. When the reader sees either of those two marks, she can anticipate what's coming.

But she cannot know what's coming—and she cannot instantly see how the second thought relates to the first—if you use any of the other marks here. The period suggests that the second thought is independent of the first. That's just not true. Parentheses suggest that the second thought is of only minor importance. Is it? Not in this case. The semicolon, depending on your reader's experience of it, could suggest all sorts of things: that the thoughts are equal in importance, that neither one deserves to be a full-fledged sentence, that they are *in some way* more intimately related than separate sentences would be, that you're beginning a list of complex ideas, and so on. While the semicolon would be correct here, it wouldn't be appropriate. Don't use a mark that disguises your intent. Use one that reveals it.

> Mr. Sadr's militia, the Mahdi Army, and the Red Jihad may begin a more open confrontation with the American military.

Do you understand that sentence to be talking about three different forces? Unless you're an expert in Middle East politics, punctuation forces that interpretation. But in fact *the Mahdi Army* is the name of Sadr's militia, and the writer's intent is to mention only two forces:

> Mr. Sadr's militia (the Mahdi Army) and the Red Jihad may begin a more open confrontation with the American military.

Parentheses come to the rescue here. They show exactly how *the Mahdi Army* relates to *Mr. Sadr's militia*. They instantly reveal that the phrase is simply another name for the same group. They're more than merely appropriate here. They're necessary for clarity. In this example, a knee-jerk prejudice against parentheses does absolutely no harm to the writer (who knows what she means), but ruins the reader's chance of understanding the writer's intent. Use whatever marks are necessary to indicate how your ideas relate.

8. Punctuation suggests how much emphasis an idea deserves.

Punctuation can do much more than clarify your meaning and show precisely how ideas fit together. It can also emphasize (and de-emphasize) particular thoughts. In the sentence below, the parenthetical phrase *to her amazement* interrupts the flow of the sentence and must be punctuated. We can punctuate it in three different ways.

commas	The medical examiner found, to her amazement, that the deceased had a diamond earring lodged in his small intestine.
parentheses	The medical examiner found (to her amazement) that the deceased had a diamond earring lodged in his small intestine.
dashes	The medical examiner found—to her amazement—that the deceased had a diamond earring lodged in his small intestine.

Each choice gives the reader a different signal about how to regard *to her amazement*. The commas merely indicate that the phrase is non-essential. They neither weaken nor strengthen emphasis. The parentheses, however, let the reader know that *to her amazement* is to be seen as nothing more than a passing thought (also called an "aside"). They de-emphasize the phrase. In contrast, the dashes call attention to it and strongly emphasize it. Now how does this work?

It works for two reasons, and the reasons are intertwined. First, we have convention, particularly with regard to parentheses. As readers, we are accustomed to seeing certain structures of language inside parentheses—the brief introduction of acronyms and abbreviations, those clarifying phrases that begin with *i.e.* and *e.g.*, short citations, and so on. Because these ideas are basically nothing more than helpful nudges, and because parentheses are customarily used to surround them, readers have come to recognize that whatever appears in parentheses is of minor importance. This recognition is part of the code of punctuation shared by readers everywhere, and you can use it to your advantage.

The same sort of recognition applies to dashes. Good writers customarily use dashes around (1) parenthetical material they want you to pay attention to or (2) material that strongly interrupts the main thought of the sentence. Nearly all readers have come to recognize that whenever the writer uses dashes, he wishes to stress an idea. This recognition may be pre-reflective or subconscious, but after all, that's what we want; we don't want our reader to scrutinize and ponder our choice of punctuation.

But along with convention, the dash has brute shape going for it. Even if your readers are unaware of the convention, they cannot help noticing ideas set off by dashes. This is primarily due to what goes on in the visual cortex when we're presented with visual stimuli. And it isn't tricky: if there are two cardinals in the tree, your focus is divided; if there is one cardinal in the tree, it receives your full attention. The rule regarding perception is that *the isolated thing is emphasized*. And when you write, the best way to emphasize anything is to isolate it, in one way or another, from the rest of the text.[6] Because the dash is the widest mark of all, it visually separates ideas more than commas or parentheses do. It creates space around the idea and thus calls your reader's attention to that idea.

As the writer, you decide how much emphasis an idea deserves. I'm not recommending that you go overboard with parentheses and dashes, but it is your responsibility to provide the appropriate signals. In the sentence below, the phrase *which is inexpensive to produce and rarely malfunctions* must be punctuated. Here are your options:

normal emphasis: The AK-47, which is inexpensive to produce and rarely malfunctions, continues to be the weapon of choice among sectarian militias.

weak emphasis:	The AK-47 (which is inexpensive to produce and rarely malfunctions) continues to be the weapon of choice among sectarian militias.
strong emphasis:	The AK-47—which is inexpensive to produce and rarely malfunctions—continues to be the weapon of choice among sectarian militias.

How do you decide which is appropriate? Remember Principle 3: since writing reflects speech, how would you *say* the idea? If you were speaking, and you dropped your voice a little, your listener would (without thinking about it) instantly understand that you intend to de-emphasize the thought. Use parentheses for that when you write. On the other hand, if you were speaking, and you suddenly paused a little longer than usual—and maybe raised your voice a little—your listener would understand that you intend to stress the idea. That's what dashes are for.

Let's examine this issue from another angle. Isn't it true that you sense a different emphasis in each of the constructions below?

Jensen did the research. Patterson wrote the report.

Jensen did the research; Patterson wrote the report.

Jensen did the research (Patterson wrote the report).

In the first example, each thought is expressed in a separate sentence. The writer is telling you that each thought should receive "sentence weight." Each thought is heavily emphasized. In the second example, the two thoughts are combined in one sentence. Here, the writer is telling you that neither thought is significant enough to receive sentence weight. As in the first example, he's telling you that the thoughts are equal in importance—but by combining them, he dilutes emphasis on each (he puts two cardinals in the tree). In the third example, the writer is telling you that who did the research is more important than who wrote the report.

Finally, let us look at the bane of readers everywhere, the over-long sentence. The following sentence was written by the director of one of the agencies in the Department of Homeland Security.

> For the past several months, documents containing errors in spelling, grammar, and punctuation have been arriving in this office for signature, and this is unacceptable, and from now on, documents containing such errors will be returned to the originator without review.

This example amply illustrates the most practical principle of sentence length: the more ideas you put into one sentence, the more you weaken emphasis on each. If you wish to taste the pepperoni, you don't complicate your pizza with anchovies and sausage. Here's the expression again, broken into smaller (more emphatic) chunks. This time you hear *This is unacceptable*; this time you sense that the writer means what he says.

> For the past several months, documents containing errors in spelling, grammar, and punctuation have been arriving in this office for signature. This is unacceptable. From now on, documents containing such errors will be returned to the originator without review.

9. Punctuation slows the reading.

The primary reasons for punctuating are to clarify and emphasize your intent, but the marks have an important side effect: they slow the reading. Both sentences below express the same thought. Why does the first one take more time to understand?

> We were unaware, until last week, that the CEO, as well as the CFO, planned to resign.

> Until last week, we were unaware that both the CEO and the CFO planned to resign.

The first sentence takes more time to grasp because *the reader has to process—make sense of—every keystroke on the page*. The haphazard order of words in the first sentence seduces the writer into using four commas. In the second sentence, the more efficient order of words requires only one. You grasp the idea more quickly because there are fewer signals to process.

You minimize the need for punctuation (and help speed the reader through the sentence) when you put words in straightforward order. Two commas are required by the helter-skelter order of words here:

> She, undeterred by the criticism, continued her research.

The more straightforward[7] constructions below require only one comma and take less time to understand.

> Undeterred by the criticism, she continued her research.

> She continued her research, undeterred by the criticism.

Now consider these. Clarity is not the issue here (all are clear). But which one do you grasp most quickly?

> Watkins visited the site and was amazed by what he saw.

> Watkins visited the site, and he was amazed by what he saw.

> Watkins visited the site; he was amazed by what he saw.

> Watkins visited the site. He was amazed by what he saw.

Comprehension time increases consistently from the first through the last. And I'm delving into this matter for two reasons. First, you always have numerous ways to express any thought, and it's essential that you know how readers react to the various alternatives. Second, you can use this reasoning to subtly influence your reader's response to your ideas. This becomes especially important when you're writing to persuade.

Most of the writing you do at work is informative. When you're writing to inform, it's a matter of courtesy to speed your reader through the ideas. You respect your reader's time when you minimize the need to punctuate—and to do that, you structure your thought in a way that doesn't require much punctuation. In the following sentence, the choice of *but* requires a comma.

> The accounting rule has been revised, but it remains open to interpretation.

In the examples below, the choice of *however*—the semantic equivalent of *but*—results in a much different treatment. This word, when used to link two sentences, requires two punctuation marks. Four constructions are possible. And because your reader has to process every keystroke on the page, each option below slows the reading to some degree.

semicolon	The accounting rule has been revised; however, it remains open to interpretation.
dash	The accounting rule has been revised—however, it remains open to interpretation.
parentheses	The accounting rule has been revised (however, it remains open to interpretation).
period	The accounting rule has been revised. However, it remains open to interpretation.

These are sensible constructions to use in persuasive writing. It's disrespectful, even pretentious, to complicate things when you're writing to inform—but when you're attempting to persuade, you want your reader to pay careful attention to the reasoning in your argument. And the way to make that happen is to *slow her down.*

I realize that's abstract. Let me give you an example. In the following paragraph, a writer at the Federal Communications Commission is supporting the Commission's decision to penalize a cellular service provider for misleading customers about how it would charge for airtime. Of particular note is the second sentence, where the writer simply lists the arguments that support his contention. Such a list requires only commas, and you can make good speed through the resulting structure.

> We believe that the reasonable consumer would not understand that the company might use anything other than the conventional cents-per-minute pricing method. There is no clear language on the rate sheets indicating otherwise, the only quoted rates are set forth in terms of minutes, and only vague references regarding the call-unit rate are provided. While the term "non-transport/non-usage charges" is used, it is not defined, and nothing in the rate sheets notifies the customer that the call-unit pricing method would be used after the promotion, or explains what that pricing method entails.

Below you'll find the same paragraph after a few minor modifications. (A few words have been added, but none have been changed.) Compare this paragraph to the first in terms of (1) the time required to read it, (2) the degree of emphasis on each supporting fact, and (3) its overall persuasiveness.

> We believe that the reasonable consumer would not understand that the company might use anything other than the conventional cents-per-minute pricing method. First, there is no clear language on the rate sheets indicating otherwise. Second, the only quoted rates are set forth in terms of minutes. Third, only vague references regarding the call-unit rate are provided. Finally, although the term "non-transport/non-usage charges" is used, it is not defined. In short, nothing in the rate sheets notifies the customer that the call-unit pricing method would be used after the promotion, or explains what that pricing method entails.

If you find the second version more convincing—as I hope you do—it's because of punctuation. This time, you can't rush through the list of supporting arguments because each one occupies a separate sentence. (The period instructs the reader to stop and process the information before going on to the next thought.) The first version contains three sentences; the revision contains six. In addition, I've added transitional words or phrases at the beginning of each sentence, and these slow you down too because they require additional punctuation. You might notice that the end of the paragraph also differs from the original. It breaks into two the long single sentence of the original, and I've done that to focus your attention on the important summarizing statement beginning with *In short*. When you have a strong argument, you want to make sure your reader recognizes it. One way to help her see it is to slow her down.

The marks take time to process, and you should use this principle to your advantage. Speed the reader through informative writing by structuring your thoughts so that they require a minimum of punctuation. In persuasive writing, structure your thoughts so that they require more time to digest.

10. Don't count too much on context to make your meaning plain.

> By some estimates, DHS is five years behind in this critical effort.

Without its context, that sentence doesn't convey anything in particular. You might guess that the writer intends *DHS* to refer to the Department of Homeland Security (and you'd be right), but you can't be certain. And you cannot guess what *this critical effort* refers to. There's simply not enough information. You'd need the context of the sentence to be sure what DHS stands for and to understand that *this critical effort* refers to ensuring the safety of the nation's food supply. Placed within that context, the sentence is a model of simplicity; stripped of context, it conveys nothing.

Context (here, simply what the reader already knows about the situation) yanks and tugs and pushes meaning in various directions. It can play a critical role in helping the reader understand your intent. Let's acknowledge that and be done with it. When we are talking about punctuation, we must look at sentences in isolation, as discrete structures of logic, because punctuation applies only to the individual sentence.

> The explosion was captured on tape by Harrison Crockbottom, a trapeze artist and a part-time clown.

Lacking context for that sentence, the reader is obligated—simply because of how the English language structures meaning—to understand that Crockbottom is a trapeze artist and a part-time clown. Meaning is encoded precisely as it is in the examples below, where there can be no doubt that Panza, Sudstrom, and Moran are being described:

> The article was written by Jack Panza, a professional football player and an avid stamp collector.

> Investigators are now focusing on Ann Sudstrom, a retired physics professor and a grandmother of eight.

> They have hired Auguste Moran, an expert cryptologist and a fluent Arabic speaker.

But I would like to take a minute to explore the limits of what context can accomplish. Suppose you live in a small town and are writing a story for the newspaper of that town. Suppose that the mayor of the town is named Harrison Crockbottom and that all of your readers know it. Suppose that a circus is visiting the town on the Sunday evening when the munitions factory (the town's major employer) explodes. Here's the sentence again.

> The explosion was captured on tape by Harrison Crockbottom, a trapeze artist and a part-time clown.

The structure of language has not changed. But *referents* have. By "referent" I mean simply *what something refers to*. Readers familiar with the context outlined above would understand that Crockbottom is not being described as a sometimes-funny acrobat. Given that background knowledge, and a little common sense, your intended readers are going to understand that sentence to mean what you want it to mean: that the explosion was videotaped by three people.

All would be well if the story ended there. It doesn't. An investigation suggests that the explosion may have been deliberate. A reporter at the *New York Times* receives an anonymous phone call from an individual claiming responsibility and saying that he acted on behalf of the victims of handgun violence. Suddenly your small town is swarming with reporters. And now your story, with your original sentence in it, is picked up by a wire service and distributed to papers nationwide. Readers of the *Los Angeles Times* and the *Baltimore Sun* have never heard of Harrison Crockbottom. They don't know he is the mayor. All they know is what they read, and what they read is what you give them. And what you give them is that he's a trapeze artist and a part-time clown.

This example is extreme, but it makes the point that you should not rely overmuch on context to make a sentence's meaning plain. Punctuation could help:

> The explosion was captured on tape by Harrison Crockbottom, a trapeze artist, and a part-time clown.

But even if you punctuate that way, the sentence remains ambiguous, and readers outside your small town are going to guess at your intention. Some will assume that Harrison Crockbottom is a trapeze artist in the same way that the cousin is a pole-vaulter in *My cousin, a pole-vaulter, won a gold medal in the Olympics*. This brings us back to Principle 1: use as many words as your meaning requires and put those words in the right order. Punctuation supplies the final polish:

> The explosion was captured on tape by Mayor Crockbottom and two members of the circus (a trapeze artist and a part-time clown).

Let's put all this into perspective. It would be absurd to demand that every expression be perfectly clear, without context, to any possible reader. When you write at work, you are not writing to all possible readers, but to a much more defined audience, and that audience has some background knowledge at its disposal.

For example, taken in isolation, the heading *Preliminary Design Review* is ambiguous to most readers, who can't be sure whether it means a preliminary review of the design or a review of the preliminary design. But the contracting officer reading the proposal knows instantly that it means the latter. She knows this because in her profession *preliminary design review* is a term of art (a use of words unique to a profession). She recognizes *preliminary design* as a unit of thought. And therefore, I think it would be overly fastidious to insist that a "clearer" way to write it is to hyphenate: *Preliminary-Design Review*. The only people whom the hyphen would assist are people who are not reading the document.

I am not advocating that you sweat over every sentence as though it were going to be immortalized in marble. I know you don't have time for that. But you do have time to *anticipate possible ambiguities* in your structures of language and to rephrase those when you revise. Don't count too much on context to make your meaning plain.

11. Know the difference between restrictive and non-restrictive expressions.

If you place a comma outside closing quotation marks, you have broken a rule in American English. Your readers may or may not know the rule, and they may or may not notice the error. Even if they do notice the error, the meaning of your expression is not obscured by that misplaced comma. I would characterize such an error as one of "form": while it will distract some readers, it does no great harm to clarity.

But when a writer inaccurately punctuates restrictive and non-restrictive expressions, much more than form is at stake. Here we are talking about meaning. And in workplace writing, this is without doubt the most common source of serious error in punctuation.

The good news is that if you know how to recognize a parenthetical expression, you know how to handle non-restrictive stuff. For practical purposes, "non-restrictive" and "parenthetical" mean exactly the same thing, and the structures are handled in exactly the same way.

Let's begin by looking at a simple construction. Of the two expressions below, one makes logical sense.

> Employees, who have not yet given blood, are encouraged to do so.

> Employees who have not yet given blood are encouraged to do so.

The second version is what you mean. The first is illogical, because the commas around *who have not yet given blood* signal that the phrase could be cut. But if we cut the phrase from the sentence, we end up with *Employees are encouraged to do so*. That's a grammatically complete thought, sure, but it isn't what the writer intends to convey.

In this example, *who have not yet given blood* is a *restrictive* idea. What that means is that the phrase serves to restrict, or limit, meaning. In this example, we are not talking about all employees. We are restricting the reference to the employees who haven't yet given blood. No commas (or any other punctuation) should surround this phrase. Every word is necessary to the writer's primary intent.

This next example is a little more complex.

> The guidance system developed by Barrioc does not rely on GPS targeting.

> The guidance system, developed by Barrioc, does not rely on GPS targeting.

Which one is right? Well, they both are. That is to say, both are correct *in form*. But they have different meanings and are appropriate in different circumstances.

Case 1

The writer is discussing more than one guidance system. He may be discussing two, or a dozen, or a hundred. If he's discussing more than one, then the phrase *developed by Barrioc* is restrictive because it specifies which guidance system does not rely on GPS targeting. In this case, the phrase is not punctuated.

Case 2

The writer has been discussing only one guidance system, and he now decides to indicate who created it. For one reason or another, he chooses not to write, as a separate sentence, *The guidance system was developed by Barrioc*. Instead, he decides to insert that idea as a minor point. He makes it parenthetical, or non-restrictive. In this case, the phrase must be punctuated.

You punctuate the expression when it is non-restrictive (when it isn't necessary to your meaning and could be cut from the sentence without damaging your intent).

"Dizzy" is non-restrictive: Oblomov's novel, *Dizzy*, won the National Book Award.

This is what you write when Oblomov has written only one novel, and (by the way) the title of the novel is *Dizzy*. In this case, *Dizzy* is non-restrictive because it does not serve to specify which novel won the award, but simply adds a bit of information. The commas around *Dizzy* make plain that the word could be cut. If it were cut, you'd have *Oblomov's novel won the National Book Award*. And that would be your primary intention if Oblomov has written one novel.

You omit punctuation to signal the reader that a word or phrase is restrictive (necessary to your intention because it identifies or specifies something).

"Dizzy" is restrictive: Oblomov's novel *Dizzy* won the National Book Award.

Given the code of meaning in English, this example indicates that Oblomov has written more than one novel, and that you are specifying which of his novels you're talking about. In that case, the absence of punctuation around *Dizzy* tells us that the word cannot be cut from the sentence because it *restricts* the meaning of *novel*.

◆ ◆ ◆

In the examples below, notice how punctuation affects meaning. In the first, *completed yesterday* is restrictive; it specifies which assessment you're talking about. (You'd need to do this if there had been more than one assessment.) The phrase is necessary for meaning and therefore is not punctuated. In the second example, *completed yesterday* merely indicates when the assessment was completed. This is the one you write when (1) there's been only one assessment or (2) the reader already knows which assessment you're discussing.

"Completed yesterday" specifies an assessment:	The assessment completed yesterday indicates that the base remains vulnerable to attack.
"Completed yesterday" merely adds information:	The assessment, completed yesterday, indicates that the base remains vulnerable to attack.

◆ ◆ ◆

Because this matter is important, and because lots of writers wrestle with it, I'm going to give some additional examples.

◆ ◆ ◆

Since there are many commissions in the world, I need to specify the one I'm talking about when I introduce it. Thus, in the example below, *formed to explore the ethics of human cloning* is restrictive—necessary to my intended meaning—and I do not punctuate it.

The commission formed to examine the ethics of human cloning will convene next week in Geneva.

But since there is only one *Aldus Commission*, the phrase *formed to investigate the ethics of human cloning* is non-restrictive—it merely adds information that could be cut—and so I punctuate it.

> The Aldus Commission, formed to examine the ethics of human cloning, will convene next week in Geneva.

◆ ◆ ◆

You must handle this matter with care because, as we've seen, a sentence can look clear to the reader but not convey your intent. In the examples below, notice how the commas (after *Republicans* and *employees*) change the meaning.

All Republicans pressured the President:	The President came under pressure from Republicans, who wanted him to do more to crack down on illegal immigration.
Only certain Republicans pressured the President:	The President came under pressure from Republicans who wanted him to do more to crack down on illegal immigration.
The policy is unfair to all SAB employees, because they all speak English as a second language:	The policy is unfair to South Asia Bureau employees, for whom English is a second language.
The policy is unfair only to the SAB employees who speak English as a second language:	The policy is unfair to South Asia Bureau employees for whom English is a second language.

12. Respect the distinction between *that* and *which*.

I want to explain this distinction because it bewilders a lot of people. Ultimately, clarity hinges more on punctuation than on this choice of words.

In everyday English, we use *which* in a number of ways. We ask a question with it: *Which proposal should we accept?* We use it to indicate that there are alternatives: *She has not decided which candidate to support.* We often use it as part of a prepositional object: *Here's his affidavit, in which he claims to have been 50 miles away at the time of the crime.* And we use it to combine two sentences when we want to subordinate[8] one:

> *HOX-51, which disposes people to behave in odd and playful ways, has been nicknamed "the goofiness gene."*

It's the last usage that gives everyone fits. That's a shame, because the matter really is fairly simple: *when you combine two sentences to make one thought less important than the other, use* which—*and don't neglect to punctuate.* Consider this example:

> The Environmental Protection Agency has a mandate to protect the environment.
>
> The Environmental Protection Agency was established in 1970.

Suppose you've written those two thoughts. Right now, each thought has sentence weight; the reader understands that they are equally important. If you intend to indicate that one is less significant than the other, you subordinate. You can subordinate either thought. Note how *which* is used for this purpose, and notice the punctuation:

subordinating the inception date:	The Environmental Protection Agency, which was established in 1970, has a mandate to protect the environment.
subordinating the mandate:	The Environmental Protection Agency, which has a mandate to protect the environment, was established in 1970.

What's essential to understand is that when you subordinate an expression this way, you make it parenthetical—it is never restrictive, and it requires punctuation.

Let's look at another example. Suppose you've written the following two sentences:

The National Institutes of Health (NIH) is headquartered in Bethesda.

NIH comprises 21 institutes.

If you intend to show the reader that one thought is less important than the other, just combine the sentences. Note the use of *which* and the punctuation:

subordinating the location:	NIH, which is headquartered in Bethesda, comprises 21 institutes.
subordinating the number of institutes:	NIH, which comprises 21 institutes, is headquartered in Bethesda.

Now let's turn to the word *that*. This word also has a number of uses in everyday English. But the important one in this discussion is its use to *specify* or *identify* something. Since there are many institutes at NIH, use *that* to specify the one you're talking about. In the examples below, the restrictive expressions are in italics.

specifying NCI:	The institute *that receives the most funding each year* is the National Cancer Institute.
specifying NIMH:	The institute *that creates the most controversy* is the National Institute of Mental Health.

Use *that* (never *which*) when you are specifying something. When you specify, the expression is restrictive—it is required for your meaning and is never punctuated.

The next two sentences are handled perfectly. The first specifies—with *that*—because there are many committees in the world and it must identify the committee it's talking about. The second subordinates *The Senate Ethics Committee convened last night*. It uses commas and *which*.

specifying a particular committee:	The committee *that has jurisdiction here* is the Senate Ethics Committee.
There is only one Senate Ethics Committee:	The Senate Ethics Committee, *which convened last night*, voted to censure the gentleman from Pennsylvania..

And now let us cut to the bone. When you use *which* without punctuation, you are begging for trouble, because this is what we get:

Do they oppose raising all taxes, or only certain taxes?	They oppose raising taxes which will harm the poor.
Are only certain handguns banned in D.C.?	The law restricts the sale of handguns which are banned in D.C.
Are all such stem cells attractive, or only certain ones?	Hematopoietic stem cells which are easily accessible and have the potential for long-term expression are an attractive target for research.

In each case, the burden of making sense has shifted to the reader. In each case, the reader cannot know whether you intend to specify or to subordinate. The absence of punctuation suggests that you intend to specify, but the presence of *which* suggests that you intend to subordinate and have neglected to punctuate. Here's what to do:

They oppose raising only certain taxes:	They oppose raising taxes that will harm the poor.
They oppose raising all taxes, and their refusal to raise taxes will harm the poor:	They oppose raising taxes, which will harm the poor.
All handguns are banned in D.C.:	The law restricts the sale of handguns, which are banned in D.C.
Only certain handguns are banned in D.C.:	The law restricts the sale of handguns that are banned in D.C.

| *All hematopoietic stem cells are attractive:* | Hematopoietic stem cells, which are easily accessible and have the potential for long-term expression, are an attractive target for research. |
| *Only certain hematopoietic stem cells are attractive:* | Hematopoietic stem cells that are easily accessible and have the potential for long-term expression are an attractive target for research. |

This matter has become complicated only because of the tendency of many writers to toss a comma in where it doesn't belong. Here's what I mean:

> The missile which was launched from 800 miles away, exploded before it reached its target.

This happens a lot. Some writers apparently believe that after nine or ten words they might need to breathe, and so they insert a comma. But when I punctuate like that—for no logical reason—I give the reader a mixed signal. I've made an error in one of two places in that sentence: either I forgot to include the comma after *missile* (a comma there would mean there's only one missile), or I should not have put the comma after *away* (if there are two or more missiles and I intend to specify a particular one). The reader can't know; context may or may not clarify my intent.

British and American usages differ here. In British English, *which* is often used to introduce a restrictive expression. In the sentences below, assume that the writer intends to specify a particular act, car, and burial chamber.

> The Act *which was passed by the House of Commons yesterday* will increase the VAT.

> The vehicle *which the police are seeking* is a red 2009 Mini Cooper with white stripes on the bonnet.

He explored the burial chamber *which was reserved for the Pharaoh's concubines.*

American usage requires *that* in such sentences. Since there is some disagreement on this issue, I suppose I'd better say that this is my preference. But it's my preference *as a reader*, because as a reader I prefer meaning made plain.

Often you can convey your intent without using either that *or* which*.*

In the examples below, notice how punctuation alone does the job.

We've received more than one report, but I'm discussing the one we received this morning:	The report received this morning confirms her hunch.
We've received only one report, and by the way, it arrived this morning:	The report, received this morning, confirms her hunch.

Those are examples of what's called "whiz-deletion" (where the writer omits either *which* or *that*). A number of authorities frown on this construction—and you'll be happy to learn that an equal number of authorities insist it's the cat's meow. Personally I find it useful in such sentences as the ones below, where punctuation suffices to show whether an idea is restrictive or merely parenthetical.

omitting "which is":	NIH, headquartered in Bethesda, comprises 21 institutes.
omitting "which are":	These theories, hotly contested by academics, are of no interest to the layman.
omitting "that are":	Applications received after September 30 will not be considered.

omitting "that was":	The species discovered in Panama has been a boon to medicine.

We have the tools we need for clarity. It makes sense to use them. Use *which* to introduce non-restrictive stuff; use *that* to introduce restrictive stuff. And don't forget to punctuate when you use *which*.

13. When is punctuation optional?

At the outset I had better address the confusion surrounding the word "optional."[9] When we are speaking about structures of language, it is a grave mistake to believe that *optional* means "it's correct either way, both with or without punctuation." That is occasionally true of emphasis; it is never true of meaning. Punctuation is not optional in the sentences below.

The suspect who has a shaky alibi has fled the country.

The suspect, who has a shaky alibi, has fled the country.

It's true that both expressions are correct in form, but we must remember our strict definition of the word "correct." *No sentence is correct unless it embodies your intention.* The expressions differ in meaning and are not interchangeable.

There is more than one suspect, and "who has a shaky alibi" specifies a certain one:	The suspect who has a shaky alibi has fled the country.
There is only one suspect, and "who has a shaky alibi" is merely parenthetical:	The suspect, who has a shaky alibi, has fled the country.

In those examples, *who has a shaky alibi* is either restrictive or non-restrictive. The same is true of *launched in October* in the following sentences. The expressions differ in meaning.

restrictive, specifying a particular satellite:	The satellite launched in October has developed a relay malfunction.
non-restrictive, adding extra information; the main thought is "The satellite has developed a relay malfunction":	The satellite, launched in October, has developed a relay malfunction.

Readers are intelligent, but they are not clairvoyant, and it is wrong to expect them to read the writer's mind. In all of the examples given, whether we punctuate or omit punctuation depends on our meaning. *Punctuation is not optional when brute meaning requires it.*

Punctuation is not optional in the following sentences either:

By June, Smith should be finished with the design.

While we ate, Professor Di Aria lectured on the significance of names.

When he ran over, his wife stopped shouting.

In the first sentence, a comma is required to prevent initially misreading *June Smith* as someone's name. In the second, a comma is required to prevent any suggestion of cannibalism. In the third, a comma is required after *over* to forestall notions of vehicular homicide. *Punctuation is not optional when clarity requires it.*

◆ ◆ ◆

Emphasis is a different matter. There are plenty of occasions when you get to decide whether your intended emphasis is best served by using or omitting punctuation. And here, an informed judgment is crucial. Omit punctuation around non-essential words and phrases when (1) the absence of punctuation would cause no confusion *and* (2) you want only *mild* emphasis on the non-essential words.

Let's remember that punctuation slows things down. Let's also remember that when you intend to emphasize something, you isolate it. Finally, let's remember that clarity is the chief goal in writing, and that when clarity doesn't require punctuation, we can omit it. With all of that in mind, consider the pairs of expressions below. All are correct, but they differ in emphatic value.

> We have in fact already committed the funds.
>
> We have, in fact, already committed the funds.
>
> Let's turn now to the philosophical problem posed by this new science.
>
> Let's turn, now, to the philosophical problem posed by this new science.
>
> The evidence was obtained illegally and therefore is inadmissible.
>
> The evidence was obtained illegally and, therefore, is inadmissible.

Each sentence contains a non-essential word or phrase that interrupts the flow of the thought. In the first sentence of each pair, I am instructing my reader to regard these interruptions as *mild*. I do not wish to emphasize them, so I do not punctuate around them. In the second sentences, I punctuate around them—isolate them—because I want you to pay a bit more attention to them. The distinctions are subtle, but important. Here's where the writer's discretion calls the shots.

At the beginning of the sentence, use judgment.

There is a growing tendency to omit the comma after one-word introductory expressions. You can omit the comma when the first word of the sentence indicates an outcome:

> Accordingly we find that the company has satisfied the letter of the law.
>
> Therefore we are returning your application unread.
>
> Thus they have failed to fulfill the contract's requirements.

Until fairly recently, convention required a comma after *Accordingly, Therefore,* and *Thus* in those examples. That comma has become discretionary, but remember—if you intend to emphasize the idea, punctuate it; omit the comma only when you want the reader to pay little attention to the transitional word.

You can omit the comma after an introductory word involving frequency:

Sometimes they sue for no reason at all.

Occasionally his manager changes "glad" to "happy."

Frequently we see cooperation between species.

Twice they have made the mistake of underestimating the competition.

You can omit the comma after many *short* introductory phrases:

This time we are using a slightly different formula.

By March they should be finished with the construction.

Quite frankly I see no reason to abandon the project.

For twenty years they have attempted to model investors' behavior.

Use a comma after longer introductory phrases:

By the end of October, we will complete Phase II.

As a result of wet weather, the deadline has been extended for three weeks.

From their point of view, our demands are arbitrary.

According to the survey, most people would not want to be anyone else.

For the sake of argument, let's pretend that everyone understands "subsequent to."

Use a comma after *First, Second, Next,* and so forth when these introductory words provide coherence:

> First, management must understand and support Plain Language. Second,
> employees who represent us to the public must be trained in what Plain
> Language requires. Third, we need to rewrite all of our boilerplate so that
> it's easy to read. Finally, we need to audience-test the new documents to
> make sure they convey what we intend to convey.

In the middle of the sentence, use judgment.

Here we are dealing with whether to punctuate a word or phrase that
interrupts the thought. As always, clarity trumps considerations of emphasis.

In the examples below, punctuation is not optional; clarity requires
it. Just imagine the sentences without the commas, and you'll see what
I mean.

> This error, in the consensus of the Board, could have been avoided.

> The black hole, in her opinion, is nature's way of reminding us who's in
> charge.

> Blotchy red patches, on the other hand, are usually not serious.

But when clarity doesn't require punctuation, let emphasis guide
you. Consider the different emphasis on *to some degree* in two versions
of the sentence below.

> *emphasizing "to some degree":* We are dealing here with words and
> phrases that, to some degree, interrupt
> the flow of thought.

> *mild emphasis on the phrase:* We are dealing here with words and
> phrases that to some degree interrupt
> the flow of thought.

Remember the principles we've already established: punctuation slows the reading, and you emphasize an idea by isolating it. Note the different emphases below:

emphasizing "with the major exception of Japan":	The year 2006 was generally positive for the Asia Pacific region, which, with the major exception of Japan, enjoyed robust economic growth.
mild emphasis on the phrase:	The year 2006 was generally positive for the Asia Pacific region, which with the major exception of Japan enjoyed robust economic growth.

Some authorities insist that the first version (with the two additional commas) is old-fashioned. While it's true that commas are omitted more frequently than they used to be, the physics of emphasis has not changed one iota. Don't omit your commas in order to prove that you're "with it" or because that's your "style." Omit them when you intend only mild emphasis on an idea.

Here are a few more examples of word order where punctuation is optional in the middle of the sentence.

emphasizing "therefore":	We have, therefore, decided to withdraw our bid.
mild emphasis on "therefore":	We have therefore decided to withdraw our bid.
emphasizing "until this morning":	They were unaware, until this morning, that the policy had changed.
mild emphasis on the phrase:	They were unaware until this morning that the policy had changed.
emphasizing "from time to time":	Food inspections have, from time to time, been less than thorough.

mild emphasis on the phrase: Food inspections have from time to time
been less than thorough.

At the end of the sentence, don't set off a prepositional phrase with a comma.

You don't have an option here. Our code for meaning dictates that sentence-ending phrases are essential to the writer's intent, even though the sentence would be technically complete without them. The examples below should strike you as childish:

He placed the classified files, on top of the safe.

Termites often nest, behind walls.

The base is surrounded, by an electrified fence.

To take the last example, it's true that *The base is surrounded* is a complete thought, but its completeness is merely grammatical. Although the phrase *by an electrified fence* is not essential to the grammatical completeness of the sentence, it is essential to the writer's intent. The same is true of every sentence-ending prepositional phrase.

When the siren sounded they hurried into the bunker.

We caught the inconsistency in the nick of time.

They were surprised by what they heard from the auditor.

We must receive the appeal by May 15.

In the interests of being thorough, I'd better mention that *occasionally* your intended emphasis is best shown when you toss this last bit of advice out the window. The comma remains taboo, but dashes and parentheses can be useful.

a dramatic and ironic outcome: When the shooting started, the people
panicked and ran—into the line of fire.

indicating that who underbid   We lost the contract because we were
you is a minor point: underbid (by Harris & Lord).

14. Use the serial comma.

Bilbo nibbled on a hot cross bun, Frodo ate a bagel, and Aragorn
devoured pancakes, hash browns, and scrambled eggs.

In that sentence, you will notice a comma after *bagel* and after *hash
browns*. A comma occupying this position (after the next-to-last item
in a list) is called the serial comma.[10] There are three distinct philoso-
phies regarding its use: always use it, never use it, and use it when you
feel like using it (also called the "it's optional" approach). The debate
over what's proper has been raging for decades. These days, nearly all
authorities—not just in the United States, but everywhere English is
spoken—advocate that you use the serial comma consistently. Most of
the exceptions appear in journalism.[11]

I used to belong to a tiny offshoot of the "it's optional" philosophy,
though I called it the "it's discretionary" view. I didn't like "optional,"
which gives the writer far too little guidance and too much leeway. The
word "discretionary" seemed more appropriate to me because it calls
for judgment. It seemed to me that the reader didn't need the serial
comma in such sentences as *The recipe calls for apples, bananas and
oranges* or *We must decide whether to pursue, amend or abandon the
application*. It seemed to me that life teaches us bananas and oranges
are different fruits, and that any intended reader of the second sentence above would understand *amending* and *abandoning* to be different activities. But experience has convinced me that most writers balk
at having to use their judgment more than is absolutely necessary. Furthermore, it's all too easy to make errors in judgment.

An error in judgment, a moment's inattention, or following the
"never use it" rule can result in spectacular foolishness:

This book is dedicated to my parents, Samuel Beckett and God.

> This week's program includes interviews with Tony Blair, a 60-year-old virgin and a dildo collector.[12]

Omitting the serial comma on the assumption that your reader can read your mind results in ambiguities like these:

> He sent his resume to Dun and Bradstreet, Farber and Lloyd and Fitzgerald.

> Possible side effects include loss of appetite, difficulty sleeping, facial tics and twitches and tremors.

In the first example, did he send a resume to a firm named *Farber and Lloyd* or to one named *Lloyd and Fitzgerald*? In the second example, we don't know for sure how many things might happen to one's face. A comma after *tics* would clarify that only the tics occur in the face. A comma after *twitches* would clarify that one's face is in danger of both tics and twitches.

Omitting the serial comma out of sheer principle is just plain wrongheaded. Here's a typical example from the *Washington Post*:

> Students are leaving college with more debt than ever, now that more of them have to rely on loans, tuition keeps rising and credit cards are being pushed on many campuses.

Readers need—deserve—the comma after *rising*. Unless you got lucky, you had to read the simple expression twice to get the intent. In this case, the writer wants us to understand he's listing three ideas following from *now that*. But on first reading, what's to prevent the reader from thinking that *now that more of them have to rely on loans* is parenthetical? Such a reading makes perfect sense too—at first. In my opinion, such writing is not good enough. Sadly, what provokes misreadings is an editorial position on style.

Sometimes, even when you use the serial comma, the result is unclear.

> Mr. Oglethorpe's will stipulates that his estate be divided equally among his wife, his brother, and his two daughters.

Here we have a serial comma after *brother*. That's fine, but put yourself in the position of the attorneys who represent each party. If you're the attorney for the wife or the brother, you argue that Mr. Oglethorpe clearly intended a three-way split (so that your client receives one-third of the estate). This would mean, of course, that each daughter would receive only one-sixth of the estate. If you represent either of the daughters, you snort at this and argue that Mr. Oglethorpe obviously intended a four-way split, so that your client receives one-quarter of the estate. This is a reasonable interpretation too, and it generates a heftier fee.

The two interpretations have equal merit, and Mr. Oglethorpe's four heirs will probably watch in dismay as costly lawsuits erode whatever inheritance they eventually get. The problem here is not with the use (or omission) of the serial comma, but with a lazy order of words. Remember Principle 1: punctuation can't overcome lackadaisical order of words. We could make the sentence mean either thing, but we'd need to recast it. Why not say what you mean? The revisions below are examples, but notice that the serial comma plays a crucial role in the first.

> Mr. Oglethorpe's will stipulates that his estate be divided equally among his wife, his brother, his daughter Lydia, and his daughter Margaret.

> Mr. Oglethorpe's will stipulates that his estate be divided as follows: one-third to his wife, one-third to his brother, and one-sixth to each of his two daughters.

The serial comma is always correct and never detracts from the clarity of an expression. The same cannot be said of its omission. You must remember the high standard we impose on ourselves—that the sentence must be not only clear, but clear on the first reading. The most practical advice is to use the serial comma consistently unless your manager finds it an affront to decency. In that case, don't use it in your draft but try to slip it in before the document goes final.

15. When do I separate adjectives with a comma?

I have to begin this essay by stating a nasty fact: there's a lot of dis-agreement on whether a comma is necessary in a construction like *large iridescent object*. Some authorities insist we should write *large, iridescent object*. Others say that the comma isn't required there. The dispute has nothing to do with the differing conventions of U.S. and British English, or with formal versus casual style, or with old-fash-ioned versus contemporary usage. It stems from a misunderstanding of the two ways in which adjectives work. I'm going to explain why your reader does not need any commas in *large iridescent object* or even in *Ms. Frost's seven rare French Impressionist paintings*.

And I have to say one more thing before we begin the analysis. There comes a point where a writer simply has to have an ear for the language. The way you acquire this ear—the firm sense that *Swiss music box* sounds fine and *music Swiss box* sounds awkward—is by reading a lot of good writing.

Coordinate Adjectives

When I write *It was a cold, windy day*, "cold" and "windy" are coordinate adjectives. What this means is that there's a hidden "and" between them. The day is cold and windy. Both adjectives describe the noun equally. You could reverse their order if you wanted to, and you'd still have the same meaning. Both describe the day in the same basic way (in this case, they describe the weather). Such adjectives should be sep-arated by a comma.

It's the same with *crisp, clear style*. What I'm saying is that some-one's writing style is crisp and clear. In this case, both adjectives serve to state my opinion of a person's style, just as *cold* and *windy* above both serve to describe the weather of a particular day.

Cumulative Adjectives

When I write *I spent most of Saturday reading several difficult economic forecasts*, "several," "difficult," and "economic" are cumulative adjectives. Here, *economic* modifies *forecasts*, *difficult* modifies the phrase *economic forecasts*, and *several* modifies the phrase *difficult economic forecasts*. No commas belong between adjectives in such expressions.

It would be the same with *the CEO's three burly security guards*. Here, *security* modifies *guards*, *burly* modifies the phrase *security guards*, and *three* modifies the entire phrase *burly security guards*.

How to Distinguish Coordinate from Cumulative Adjectives

Nearly all authorities recommend that you perform two quick tests to determine whether adjectives are coordinate (and require a comma) or cumulative (and should not be separated by a comma). In many cases, these tests are useful.

THE "AND" TEST

Suppose I'm writing about *an alarming, unprecedented event*. To determine whether the adjectives are coordinate or cumulative, I imagine putting *and* between them. I would get *an alarming and unprecedented event*. That expression makes perfect sense; it sounds okay and it's another way of saying what I intend. So the two adjectives are coordinate and I should separate them with a comma.

THE "REVERSE-THE-ORDER" TEST

What if I reversed the order of those adjectives? Would the expression mean the same thing if I wrote about *an unprecedented and alarming event*? Yes, it would still have the same meaning, even though it does not sound quite as natural. So if I'm unconcerned about the awkwardness of the word order, I could write about *an unprecedented, alarming event*. If I do, I use a comma.

But this is the tricky part, because a good writer tries to avoid awkwardness. And this is where an ear for language comes in handy. Why does *little old lady* sound natural and *old little lady* sound awkward? And why is it we never see a comma in that phrase? After all, she is a *little and old lady*, so it passes the "and" test; we could say she is an *old and little lady*, so it passes the "reverse-the-order" test. So why shouldn't we write *little, old lady*? What's going on?

What's going on is that there's a conventional order of description in English. Your ear should tell you that *expensive pearl necklace* sounds like English, while *pearl expensive necklace* does not. This is because, in English, we give our assessment of something (*expensive*) before we state the material (*pearl*). We state something's size (*little*) before we state its age (*old*). And when we use the adjectives in conventional order, we do not separate them with commas.

This sequence isn't engraved in stone, but with occasional exceptions the order of description goes like this:

Article	the phone, a pencil, an owl
Ownership	her view, Wilson's point
Number	three ships, eight secrets
Impression or Opinion	formidable opponent, excellent example
Size	tiny organism, enormous mistake
Age	20-year-old policy, ancient inscription
Shape	round table, square joint
Color	blue bus, red leaf
Origin	Chinese art, lunar eclipse
Material	copper pipe, paper doll
Purpose	conference room, talking point

When I use adjectives in that order, I'm using them cumulatively, and I don't separate them with commas. Thus I write about *Sindbad's seven ridiculous voyages, shiny red plastic trombones*, a *small chocolate Belgian waffle*, and a *square aluminum roasting pan.*

If I don't follow that order of description, then I don't understand what the language requires, and commas won't help. If I write something like *We sampled her Greek delicious many pastries*, it really doesn't matter whether I use commas, because the word order is not that of English. *We sampled her many delicious Greek pastries* doesn't need commas.

Now a *grumpy old man* is one thing, and a *feisty, grumpy old man* is something else. The grumpy old man doesn't need a comma, because *grumpy* and *old* follow the order above. But *the feisty, grumpy old man* can't get around without his comma, because his *feisty* and his *grumpy* describe similar virtues of his disposition. In this case, *feisty* and *grumpy* both describe the writer's opinion of the old man. They are coordinating adjectives, and what that means is that they need to be separated either with a comma or with an "and."

That's basically all there is to it, but I'll give a few more examples to make sure you see the distinction.

Interestingly, several authorities use the sentence *Felix is a lonely, young boy* as an example of the correct use of the comma. This is wrong. No comma should be there because in *lonely young boy*, just as in *little old lady* and *grumpy old man*, the adjectives follow the established order of description. If you refer to Felix as *a frightened, lonely young boy*, sure, put a comma between *frightened* and *lonely* because those two adjectives are coordinate: both state your impression of Felix. But if you call him a *lonely young Irish boy*, don't punctuate. Those adjectives are cumulative.

The writer has a *clear, concise style*, but we see vapor trails in the *clear blue sky*. James Joyce's novel *Ulysses* begins with "Stately, plump Buck Mulligan." Mr. Mulligan is both stately and plump. You could write *plump, stately Buck Mulligan* and your reader would be equally entertained. But on the bed, without commas, are *four plump stuffed animals*. It makes no sense to write *stuffed four plump animals, four stuffed plump animals, plump stuffed four animals,* or any other order of these words.

Finally, I'm assuming that in workplace writing you'll rarely put more than two or three adjectives in front of a noun. Maybe you write of the *tedious 50-page marketing proposal,* but it seems to me that any further description would say more about you than it would about the proposal. If you write *I spent over three hours reading the wordy, sloppy, incoherent, overblown, and utterly tedious 50-page marketing proposal,* your punctuation is fine, but what the reader gets is a report on your frustration.

16. Use the hyphen to clarify "improvised usage."

If you work for Freddie Mac and you want to know whether *multifamily housing* or *multi-family housing* is preferred, you can check the corporation's style guide. At the Federal Communications Commission you can check the FCC style guide to see whether you should write *spread-spectrum analysis* or *spread spectrum analysis.* If you're unsure whether *self-obsessed* requires a hyphen (it does), you can simply check a dictionary.

But you can't look for help in style guides and dictionaries if you write something like *The utility's customer-be-damned philosophy has attracted the attention of regulators.*

You're not going to find guidance about *customer be damned* in any style guide or dictionary; it's the kind of adjective that a writer invents on the spot. Improvised usages can be effective, but they are responsible for most of the confusion (and resulting error) in the use of the hyphen.

First of all, it's important to understand that the hyphen gives you great flexibility in the order of words. This is significant because English (unlike many other languages) depends on the order of words for meaning. *The crow ate the dead rat* and *The rat ate the dead crow* consist of the same words; it's only the difference in word order that creates the different meanings.

Flexibility in word order is useful, because emphasis—how vigorously a word attracts the reader's attention—depends partly on where that word is in a sentence. The last word in a sentence is always emphatic. That's because the period instructs the reader to hesitate for an instant, and synthesize what he's just read, before going on to the next sentence. In that brief hiatus, the last word resonates. And that's why the second example below sounds just a bit more urgent.

The errors must be immediately corrected.

The errors must be corrected immediately.

What do you want to emphasize at the end of a sentence? The hyphen gives you an option. Below, the hyphenated versions put more stress on *resume* and *systems*.

All candidates must submit a resume that is up to date.

All candidates must submit an up-to-date resume.

We need better models of systems that hop frequencies.

We need better models of frequency-hopping systems.

The hyphen gives you flexibility in word order elsewhere in the sentence too. You can use it to convert phrases into shorter adjectives and put more emphasis on a particular noun. In the examples below, both *report* and *diseases* receive more emphasis when the hyphen is used, simply because using the hyphen results in fewer words to process. Another benefit is that the technique puts subject and verb side by side.

The report from the fourth quarter showed a slight increase in margin.

The fourth-quarter report showed a slight increase in margin.

As the climate warms, diseases that are spread by insects will become more widespread.

As the climate warms, insect-borne diseases will become more widespread.

Improvised usage yields conciseness, and you see examples of it everywhere you look. The quarterly report from the Dodge & Cox Stock Fund states that Federal Express has a *difficult-to-replicate* distribution service. That's a lot more concise than saying that Federal Express has a distribution service that is difficult to replicate. Wandering around the house and reading what's here, I notice that Purina One dog food has an *anti-oxidant-rich formula*, which is more economical than saying it has a formula that is rich in anti-oxidants. Fresh Step Cat Litter, I read, has *paw-activated crystals*, not crystals that are activated by the antics of your cat's paws. The milk is loaded with *bone-building calcium*. The cereal is excellent for a *low-cholesterol diet*. Not one of these usages can be found in any dictionary or style guide. All are improvised.

How do I determine whether I need to hyphenate?

There's a logical method, and it consists of several steps. First, look at the order of words in the two examples below.

hot humid day   long boring discussion

Next, let's agree that a day can be humid without being hot; it can be hot without being humid; and it can be both hot and humid. When both of the adjectives could describe the noun independently, you use a comma or an *and* between them. You write either *hot, humid day* or *hot and humid day*. The second example behaves the same way, and you'd write *long, boring discussion* or *long and boring discussion*.

Finally, we need to recognize that words are behaving differently in these expressions:

long term goal   fat free pudding   above average results

This time, the adjectives do not independently describe the noun. Instead, they form a unit of thought. You test this by imagining an *and* between them. It makes no sense to speak of a goal that is both *long* and *term*—*It is a long and term goal* isn't what you mean—and so you hyphenate, and write of the *long-term goal*. Using precisely the same logic, you write of the *fat-free pudding*. It is not *fat pudding* and *free pudding*, and if you mentally phrase the sense as *fat and free pudding*, you instantly see that's not what you intend. In the last example, we're talking about results that are above average. We cannot put an *and* in the phrase; *above and average results* is not what we mean. We mean *above-average results*.

Just in case the horse has not passed away, we have *bomb-sniffing dogs* (they are not both bomb dogs and sniffing dogs), *Chinese-made toothpaste* (it is not both Chinese toothpaste and made toothpaste), and a *hot-tempered economist* (the economist is not both *hot* and *tempered* in the way that the day is both *hot* and *humid*).

When more than one of these hyphenated adjectives precedes the noun, you need to separate them with commas.

> She's a mild-mannered, soft-spoken, prize-winning novelist.

> Her sister is a trash-talking, in-your-face, professional bull rider.

> It was a jargon-laden, impossible-to-follow report.

Some readers find this approach distractingly ugly and refer to it as "hyphen abuse." They are entitled to their epithet, but to me it makes more sense to consider the alternatives. The alternative we do *not* want is that of omitting hyphens when they are necessary for instant clarity, as would be the case in *a last minute five page addendum*. The alternative that benefits the reader is that of finding more precise words and putting those words in sensible order. Rather than write *It was a jargon-laden, impossible-to-follow report*, we might write *The report bristled with jargon and was impossible to understand*.

A Note on What People Call "the Prevailing Chaos"

The attempt to formulate coherent rules for the proper use of the hyphen drives certain people crazy. These people are primarily editors.

Probably the most famous lament comes from John Benbow, editor of the stylebook for the Oxford University Press, who said simply, "If you take hyphens seriously, you will surely go mad." The Fowler brothers, who were the first editors of the *Concise Oxford Dictionary*, had this to say in their preface to the 1911 edition:

> We have also to admit that after trying hard at an early stage to arrive at some principle that should teach us when to separate, when to hyphen, and when to unite the parts of compound words, we had to abandon the attempt as hopeless, and welter in the prevailing chaos.

The reason why editors can't create universal principles covering the use of the hyphen is not that there are no coherent principles. It's that some of these principles apply to some structures of language, but not to other, logically identical structures, and that they apply only in certain contexts, and are necessary only for particular audiences. In other words, the sheer number of variables obstructs the formulation of rule. Everyone agrees that *a last, desperate effort* requires a comma and *a last-ditch effort* requires a hyphen; everyone agrees that the phrases *law enforcement officer* and *federal budget deficit* don't require a hyphen because they are familiar and readily understood.

But there's a lot of disagreement about other constructions. For example, what's the right way to attach a prefix to a word? Should I write *re-interrogate* or *reinterrogate*? Is it better to write *co-worker* or *coworker*? In these cases, what matters is how your reader is accustomed to seeing the word spelled. Over time, and with frequent-enough use, hyphenated prefixes tend to become fused to the primary word. If you work for an organization that frequently re-interrogates people, then *reinterrogate* would instantly convey. Frankly I think *coworker* simply looks strange—it continues to make me wonder what it means to ork a cow—but after I encounter it a thousand more times, its power to dismay me will wear off. In cases of prefixes, if you are unsure, then use the hyphen. Prefer *re-enter* to *reenter* and *co-indicate* to *coindicate*.

I encourage you to do the same with phrases. When we write, we're writing to a particular audience, and we know who that audience is, and we should be able to figure out whether *combat ready troops* is what those readers are used to, or whether they need *combat-ready troops*. If you're unsure, it's best to hyphenate.

The hyphen is simply another tool we use to guide the reader's rapidly moving eye.

Your judgment should tell you that *best-case scenario* is better than *best case scenario*, even though a rule states that we do not hyphenate compounds when the first word is superlative. We are not talking about a case scenario. Nor are we necessarily talking about a majority of *admired managers* when we write *most admired managers*. We might be referring to managers who are the most admired, and in that case we must write of the *most-admired managers*.

Most-admired managers share a number of personality traits.

You're not supposed to hyphenate a compound adjective when the first word is comparative, either, but if you read *The study should yield more conclusive results*, you cannot know whether the writer means additional conclusive results or results that are more conclusive. In the latter instance, meaning requires *more-conclusive results*.

In cases of this sort, it's better to use a hyphen than to omit one just because the rules say it shouldn't be there.

We can't do much about what the rules say, but our duty is to be clear. When being clear requires that you violate a rule, violate it without a second thought. The gods of writing recognize and bless conscientious objectors. And even if they don't, the reader does. Call me wrong; accuse me of error; but don't call me unclear.

17. Sometimes, no matter how you punctuate, a reader is going to think it's wrong.

You can't please everyone all the time. The best you can do is know the conventions, follow the code of meaning supplied by those conventions, and hope that your reader goes by the same code. Ultimately, though, you can't know what "punctuation baggage" your readers bring to your text.

What people were taught by a forceful third-grade teacher clings to the mind forever—at least it does among those who don't observe how the language is actually used.[13] (That's why it's important to read well-written stuff.) Complicating this problem is that for the last 20 years, punctuation hasn't been part of the curriculum in most of the United States. Students are expected to express themselves fearlessly—something they can't do if they're at all concerned about clarity—and magically pick up the rules of punctuation on their own. This is like teaching the lesson of the gas pedal and ignoring the lesson of the brake.

Even when the issue is taught, the way it is taught might fairly be called haphazard. You have been plagued by hand-me-down guidance such as "Put in a comma where you'd pause," "Use a semicolon before *however*," and so on. You may have been taught to use the serial comma consistently, or never to use it, or that its use is optional. Teachers at all levels (from grade school through grad school) have their personal preferences and peeves regarding punctuation, and it's common to hear "Never use dashes" as a freshman and "Dashes are fine, but never use parentheses" as a sophomore. If your current manager insists on *a.m.* and *p.m.*, it's almost certain that as soon as you're promoted, your next manager will say that's absurd, and insist that *AM* and *PM* is the only civilized way to write it.

On and on it goes, the parade of pet peeves and erroneous rules: "Never put a comma in front of *that*," "Always put a comma in front of *which*," "Put a semicolon after each bullet item in a vertical list." No one reaches adulthood unscathed by this stuff.

And as though the issue weren't confusing enough, we must also contend with the profoundly asinine notion that some "styles" of punctuation are more formal than others. Formality-loving proponents of this strange philosophy contend, for example, that using semicolons to separate items in a list is more "formal" (and therefore better) than using bullets. Informality-loving proponents of the same philosophy argue that using a colon to set up a summary statement is "too formal" and should be confined to academic writing.

Let's try to remain practical. As writers, we have (1) an intention to convey and (2) various tools we can use for conveying that intention. Some tools work better than others. Sure, I can yank a nail out of a two-by-four with my teeth, but it would be more sensible to use the claw of a hammer. Withholding efficient punctuation is a grave disservice to readers, and the motive becomes fatuous when someone withholds these helpful structures because he thinks they are either too formal or too informal. Considerations of formality do not apply to the wrench and the pliers. Considerations of efficiency do.

But reason does not stop people's knees from jerking when they see a perfectly appropriate construction they were once taught is "wrong," or "weak," or "too formal," or "too informal." And what all of this means is that you can practice every commonsense technique in this book and still hear quibbling. You're not going to please all of your readers all of the time. Ultimately, whether it is "better" or "more proper" or "correct" to write *E-mail*, *e-mail*, or *email* is a religious issue, not a rational one. Let it go.

18. Feed your head.

Read well-written stuff, and you'll absorb a sense of how punctuation works and what it can accomplish. And even if these usages smolder somewhere in your subconscious, they surface in your writing, and ultimately they become habit. Your grasp of all language conventions improves when you read such periodicals as *Scientific American*, *Time*, *National Geographic*, or a big-city newspaper. It's essential that you read good writing and not confine your reading to the stuff you're forced to consume at work.

You can pick up some very bad habits from the reports, analyses, memos, and policies that lurch and stagger down the corridors of the workplace, unchanged over the years. I encourage you to bring fresh genes into the gene pool of your writing. If you don't, your style will become inbred, as it were, with particular usages (not always practical ones) seeming "right" only because they are routine. Your alternatives will shrink; your options will narrow; and in the end you will wonder why your writing seems so tedious and dull.

19. When you see an odd usage, consider the source.

What we read determines our sense of what makes language look right and sound right. Certainly this is true of our feel for punctuation. Since it's impossible to create order from all the contradictory advice tossed at us over the years, we look to what we read for practical guidance. As I've mentioned, this can be dangerous if most of what you read is the rough stuff of the workplace, because in everyday business writing you encounter punctuation that's distracting, confusing, overblown, unnecessary, and simply wrong. Don't pluck fruit from a poisoned orchard.

When you read documents written by people who lack skill with language, you often see marks misplaced, misused, and omitted in all kinds of ways. Some examples:

I need two (2) boxes, of 4 inch high density CD's.

Be sure to notify us; however, if you intend to appeal.

They have asked us to: explain why the records have been classified.

Visitors must "sign in" at the front desk and receive a badge to be worn-at-all-times.

You is Frogmorton Toyota and I is the individual(s) whose signature(s) appear(s) below.

When a usage distracts you, or simply looks odd, always consider the source. Reports written by your co-workers may not exemplify practical standards. Under deadline pressure, even individuals who should know better occasionally blow it. When headline writers neglect to punctuate, readers get headlines like these:

Hospital Sued by Seven Foot Doctors

Reader Upset over Dog Eating Filipinos

Where's the Beef Awarded Prize

Physically Challenged Individuals Insulted by Cripple

The first two examples need hyphens. The first one should have been *Foot-Doctors*, since *Podiatrists* apparently would have been unclear. The second one is clear, but backward: it should have been *Dog-Eating*, since the reader was upset over the Filipinos eating dogs. The third and fourth examples need quotation marks: *'Where's the Beef'* *Awarded Prize* and *Physically Challenged Individuals Insulted by 'Cripple.'* Now we understand that a certain slogan has received a prize and that people have been insulted by a particular word. (In headlines, single quotation marks are standard.)

In the example below, taken verbatim from the "Market Update" found on Yahoo!, note the punctuation around *Financials*:

10:00 am: The indices are holding on to the bulk of their gains as eight out of 10 sectors remain positive. A respectable 0.7% advance for the most influential sector of them all—Financials, is providing the bulk of early support.

We do need to punctuate around *Financials* because the word is parenthetical, but it's surprising to see a dash on one side of it and a comma on the other. You would never spot that construction in the *Wall Street Journal*. My point is that errors and bizarre usages abound, and particularly in hasty writing. You won't see *i.e.* used to begin a sentence in carefully edited writing, but you'll see it in a memo here and there. Don't emulate error. Consider the source.

The Marks

1. Apostrophe

We use the apostrophe to form contractions and to show ownership. The mark is used to create plural forms only when using *s* to form a plural would be confusing.

1.1 Contractions

In *They're finishing the project*, the apostrophe indicates that you've left out the *a* in *are*. In *She said she'd catch the next flight*, the apostrophe indicates the omission of *woul* in *would*. Many people consider contractions to be informal—appropriate to spoken but not to written English—but they often have a place in day-to-day workplace writing. They don't belong in rules, regulations, directives, and contracts, but they can help create a conversational tone in correspondence. Contractions are especially important in plain language texts of all sorts. Use them when the occasion calls for a relaxed or personal tone. *I'm looking forward to meeting you* is arguably better for business than *Making your acquaintance is eagerly anticipated by the undersigned*.

1.2 Possessives

When you write *Sam's boots*, you're indicating that the boots belong to Sam. Here, the apostrophe indicates the omission of *h* and *i*. *Sam's boots* is actually a contraction of *Sam his boots*. What you're saying with *Helen's idea* is *Helen his idea*.[1]

1.3 When a noun (singular or plural) ends in a letter other than s, use an apostrophe and an s to form the possessive.

one man's decision	the men's decision	IBM's policy
a woman's life	the women's section	the cacti's life span

1.4 When a singular noun ends in an s, simply add an apostrophe to form the possessive.

Jones' reaction	Hawkins' analysis	my boss' idea

People argue about this usage. Some authorities say you should add both an apostrophe and an *s* (e.g., *Dickens's novels, Jenkins's plan*). Others say that sometimes you add both an apostrophe and an *s* and sometimes you add only the apostrophe, depending on the sound. But are we really in control of what the reader imagines he hears when he reads? I'm recommending my preference here because I think most readers share it. If your organization has a style guide, consult it on this issue. If your organization has no style guide, prepare yourself for senseless arguments.

1.5 When a possessive construction looks strange to you, find another way to show ownership.

If you think that both *Aranjuez' music* and *Aranjuez's music* look odd, then write about the *music of Aranjuez*. If *Davis' findings* and *Davis's findings* both look awkward to you, then phrase the idea *the findings of Davis*. You could also write *Davis finds* or *Davis has found*.

1.6 When the plural of a noun ends in s (as most do), add only the apostrophe to form the possessive.

the employees' goal	the companies' supplier	the players' diet

1.7 When the plural of a noun does not end in s, add the apostrophe and the s to form the possessive.

the women's club   the children's toys

the criteria's focus   the data's validity

1.8 In cases where ownership is joint, only the last noun receives an apostrophe and an s.

JGT and DDI's joint proposal

O'Rourke and Creal's partnership

FBI and CIA's shared task

1.9 In cases where there is no joint ownership, make both (or all) of the nouns possessive.

JGT's and DDI's proposals are nearly identical.

EPA's and BLM's mandates sometimes conflict.

Fujita's, Walker's, and Pang's theories help explain climate change.

1.10 In compounds, make only the last noun possessive.

someone else's problem

the Attorney General's mistake

Smith & Wesson's patents

1.11 Don't use the apostrophe with possessive pronouns.

ours (not our's); yours (not your's)

theirs (not their's)

hers (not her's)

its (*it's* is a contraction of *it is* or *it has*)

1.12 Use the possessive case in expressions of duration.

The possessive case makes sense intuitively in phrases like *a moment's notice* and *last year's results*. After all, last year's results are the results "of" last year in exactly the same way Jack's boots are the boots "of" Jack.

Using the possessive may not be quite so intuitive in expressions like *a year's imprisonment* and *eight hours' work*. But the apostrophe is necessary in such expressions of duration; here, we are talking about imprisonment that lasts for a year and work that occupies eight hours. Use the apostrophe and the *s* here, and simply follow the rules regarding singular and plural, as in the examples below.

one day's effort	one week's vacation
three months' notice	five days' pay

In such expressions, you could hyphenate instead if you changed the words only slightly. For example, instead of writing about a need for three months' notice, you could say you need *a three-month notice*. Instead of saying that someone was sentenced to a year's imprisonment, you could say he received *a one-year sentence*.

1.13 Use the possessive case for a noun preceding a verb ending in ing.

Jill's seeking enlightenment led to her joining the circus.

My manager's scheming will ultimately cost him his job.

The company's establishing an office in China is a risky move.

1.14 Rarely do we use the apostrophe to form plurals.

The apostrophe plus *s* construction is used to form plurals in three special circumstances. First, use it on those rare occasions when you need to pluralize a single letter or digit:

> She has trouble pronouncing f's and v's.

> The data stream consists of 1's and 0's.

Second, use it when you are pluralizing an abbreviation that ends with a period:

> He has Ph.D.'s in linguistics and psychology.

> Nine people with M.B.A.'s have applied for the position.

Finally, use it whenever it's absolutely necessary for clarity:

> Have you considered the pro's and cons?

> The diplomat explained the do's and don'ts of the culture.

Here you simply have to trust your judgment. *Newsweek* omits the apostrophe in *pros and cons*, probably because the phrase has become a unit easily recognized by the culture. Generally speaking, it's safe to follow the lead of the editors of a mainstream periodical.

Don't use the apostrophe + *s* to form the plural in any other circumstance. When an abbreviation doesn't end with a period (most don't), just use an *s* to form the plural:

> several RFPs   12 CEOs

> some of the ATMs   a squadron of F-22s

This is also true in expressions of units of historical time. Just add an *s*.

> The stock markets of most developed nations surged during the 1990s.

Over one million Irish immigrated to the United States in the 1900s.

1.15 Think twice about using the apostrophe to abbreviate the decade, as in '20s and '60s.

The apostrophe used to be expected in such constructions as *the Roaring '20s* and *the Psychedelic '60s*. Here it indicates the omission of *19*. These days there is apparently no consensus on whether that apostrophe is required. Because context would indicate that you're discussing a decade, common sense suggests we omit the apostrophe here, especially when you consider that it leads to such constructions as *the '70's military build-up* (meaning the build-up that occurred throughout the 70s) and *the '90's economic spurt* (the spurt that occurred during the 90s). The constructions *'70's* and *'90's* would be logical there, but the ideas are clearer if we write about *the military build-up of the 70s* and *the economic spurt of the 90s*.

1.16 Be exact with the names of organizations, places, and institutions.

Always follow the "authentic" form (the conventional way the name has come to be handled). *Harpers Ferry*, for example, was named for a place where a fellow named Harper once operated a ferry, and thus an English teacher would want to call it *Harper's Ferry* (using the apostrophe to indicate ownership). But the authentic form of the name (the way the name is expressed in the town charter and on all maps) lacks the apostrophe—and you should follow that lead. It is the same with *Typesetters Union, Dramatists Guild, Johns Hopkins University*, and in every other case where names have become descriptive, rather than possessive.

The other side of this rule is that we should use the apostrophe when the name of the organization, place, or periodical conventionally uses one. It is *Reader's Digest*, for example, not *Readers' Digest* or *Readers Digest*. Why? Simply because that's how *Reader's Digest* prefers it.

2. Brackets   [ ]

Brackets are tricky marks to use well. First I'll explain what they're for and show you a few examples. But then we'll take a hard look at the limits of their usefulness. Often, the mere fact that brackets are required suggests that the writer may not have used good judgment.

2.1 Brackets are used only with quotations.

When you're quoting, and you comment within the quoted material, use brackets to show that your remark isn't part of the original quotation.

The reader assumes that quotations are sacred; in other words, she assumes that whatever you put inside quotation marks is verbatim—unchanged—from the source. That's the deal. Because this is the case, you have to confess every time you tinker with the words of a quotation. You confess inside brackets. Think of them as a little confessional box.

Suppose I wish to quote someone who wrote, "The merger will harm the employees of the smaller company." Those are the writer's words, and I am ethically obliged not to change them. But if I have reason to believe that my readers won't know what the writer meant by "the smaller company"—if context doesn't make that plain—then I need to clarify the matter, and I might use brackets for the purpose. The result looks like this:

> "The merger will harm the employees of the smaller company [Ardent]."

Including *Ardent* identifies the company. What the brackets do is signal the reader that *Ardent* was not part of the original quotation.

2.2 Use brackets when you insert clarifying remarks in a quotation.

When quoting, we sometimes need to insert a word or phrase to clarify things for the reader.

if, without context, the word "they" would be vague:	The analyst remarked, "No one knows whether they [the Chinese Central Bank] will raise interest rates."
if you believe the reader is unfamiliar with "IEDs":	The Pentagon spokesman said, "Yesterday alone, nine IEDs [improvised explosive devices] were discovered in a 2-mile stretch of the road."

2.3 Use brackets when you substitute a word or phrase in a quotation.

In 2.2, clarifying words are *added* in brackets. The original quotation is left intact. Another approach consists of *substituting* clearer words in brackets—and eliminating the unclear terms. I'd recommend that you confine this approach to quoting spoken language.

Speakers aren't as deliberate as writers; we often say things we would never write. As speakers, we put words in the wrong order, clutter our phrasing, and butcher grammar. Suppose you're quoting someone who said, "I want my employees to be able to communicate well, both orally and writtenly."

You have a decision to make. You can do one of four things with this quotation.

verbatim:	The director said, "I want my employees to be able to communicate well, both orally and writtenly."
with a sic:	The director said, "I want my employees to be able to communicate well, both orally and writtenly [*sic*]."[2]
a paraphrase:	The director said he wanted his employees to be able to communicate well, both when they speak and when they write.

substituting a better phrase:	The director said, "I want my employees to be able to communicate well, both orally and [when they write]."

The first two options make the speaker look foolish. The second option underscores the speaker's foolishness; it could also suggest a smug superiority on your part. The third option removes all traces of foolishness, though you sacrifice the sense of exactness supplied by quoting. The fourth option—which is what we're talking about here—may leave a few readers wondering what the director actually said, but most readers are content to get the gist of it in plain words. Note how we use brackets to indicate that *when they write* takes the place of what the director actually said.

Now in that example, we're replacing bad grammar. Sometimes, as in the next example, experts use terms that wouldn't be clear to your audience. In such cases, you might use brackets to replace the technical terms with everyday words:

the original:	"Left ventricular infarctions can be prevented by pharmacologic therapeutics."
the gist of it:	"[Heart attacks] can be prevented by [drug therapy]."

Sometimes, even when people don't use technical terms, they simply use overly difficult words. Again, you might clarify the intent by substituting, in brackets, an ordinary word:

the original:	"It's essential to nexus your arguments."
the gist of it:	"It's essential to [link] your arguments."

Stop—let's consider what the reader really needs.
What I've just shown you is how to use brackets when you either insert or substitute clarifying words in a quotation. This is the *correct* use of brackets, but being correct doesn't always equate to being readable. You should use brackets for this purpose only when you can't find a less intrusive way to clarify your meaning, because the practice can easily result in cumbersome expressions.

Here's an extreme example of cumbersome use of bracketed phrases:

> "Lieutenant!" Colonel Yeager shouted. "Take that APC [armored personnel carrier] to the BARF [best available retrofit facility]! And bring me some new LPCs [leather personnel carriers, also known as "boots"] on the way back!"

If a quote needs that much help, it's probably best not to use it at all—unless you're using it to make a comic point. Nearly always, you serve your reader best when you find a less interruptive way to clarify an unclear reference.

instead of:	The analyst remarked, "No one knows whether they [the Chinese central bank] will raise interest rates."
try this:	Speaking of the Chinese central bank, the analyst remarked, "No one knows whether they will raise interest rates."
instead of:	The Pentagon spokesman said, "Yesterday alone, nine IEDs [improvised explosive devices] were found in a 2-mile stretch of the road."
paraphrase:	The Pentagon spokesman said that yesterday alone, nine makeshift explosive devices were found in a 2-mile stretch of the road.

If your goal is not to increase the reader's technical vocabulary, then your reader doesn't need to encounter technical terms. All he needs is to get the gist of the thought. When faced with language so highly specialized as *Left ventricular infarctions can be prevented by pharmacologic therapeutics,* does it really make sense to use brackets and write, "[Heart attacks] can be prevented by [drug therapy]"? Isn't it better to admit that the original sentence is simply not a good candidate for a quote when you're writing to non-experts? In such cases, your reader benefits when you paraphrase.

In the example below, assume that the important point—the reason you're quoting the sentence in the first place—is that NASA has not yet decided on a design, but is still considering various designs.

instead of inserting a phrase in brackets:	The NASA spokesman said, "We are considering several designs for the space station's dexterous mechanical end effector [robotic hand]."
or substituting a phrase in brackets:	The NASA spokesman said, "We are considering several designs for the space station's [robotic hand]."
quote only the essential phrase:	The spokesman said that NASA is "considering several designs" for the space station's robotic hand.

2.4 Use brackets with sic.

As a reader, you've probably noticed the device *sic* in a quotation. It always goes inside brackets. *Sic* is a Latin word meaning "thus." Its practical meaning is *This is the way it was in the original quotation.* Use it *immediately after an error* in the mechanics of language (spelling, punctuation, grammar, etc.) in the original.[3] Note that it's italicized.

> The executive wrote, "Unless we increase advertising, we will loose [*sic*] market share."

> The article concluded, "Climate change is real, but it's [*sic*] impact is unclear."

Be careful with this practice. If you overuse *sic*, readers wonder about your motives—they begin wondering about things that have nothing to do with your point. In plain words, they may wonder whether you're a sarcastic smart aleck. Unless you're making a point about how utterly sloppy a piece of writing is, avoid this:

> The advertisement reads, "Our new homes eximplify [*sic*] the new tardition [*sic*] in todays [*sic*] simplistic architecture."

2.5 Don't use parentheses if the meaning requires brackets.

Parentheses and brackets have entirely different functions. The writer uses parentheses; only the editor uses brackets. You cannot expect your reader to know that you have added the judge's name if you write, *According to the article, "The judge (Oscar Mayne) grew noticeably impatient with the delay."* Only brackets would indicate that you've added the words.

2.6 Don't use brackets inside parentheses.

The result may make sense logically, but it's usually difficult to understand. If you really need to "nest" one parenthetical expression inside another, the time has come to rethink your choice of words or to use a footnote. The decision to use *UAV* is what causes all the trouble here:

> Commanders in the field are clamoring for more UAVs (unmanned aerial vehicles, a species of drone [pilotless aircraft operated by remote control] that can either provide "persistent stare capability" [constant video surveillance of an area] or carry missiles) in Afghanistan and Iraq.

That expression conforms to all the rules of English, but no one would call it good writing. Compassion for the reader requires that we revise the expression. Here's an example of how you might recast it:

> Commanders in Afghanistan and Iraq are clamoring for more drones (aircraft operated by remote control). Without risking a pilot's life, drones can not only provide constant video surveillance of a battlefield, but can carry missiles and be used as weapons.

If one of your goals is to acquaint your reader with what a UAV is, then you need more words.

> Commanders in Afghanistan and Iraq are clamoring for more UAVs (unmanned aerial vehicles). Like all drones, UAVs are operated by remote control. Without risking a pilot's life, they can not only provide constant video surveillance of a battlefield, but can carry missiles and be used as weapons.

3. Colon :

Use a colon to announce a summary statement, to introduce a list, to express ratio, or to follow a salutation line.

3.1 Use a colon between two sentences when the second sentence answers the question raised by the first.

When your first independent clause raises a question and the next one answers that question, the second clause is called a "summary statement." Use a colon to introduce it. For example, if I write *I have one objection to this report*, the reader naturally wonders, "What's your objection?" When I raise a question, I'm obliged to answer it right away, and I could do it like this: *I have one objection to this report: it is far too technical for its intended audience.*

> The argument is suspect: it relies more on faith than on actual observation.

> She is well qualified to serve as ambassador: she is a 12-year veteran of the embassy, fluent in Russian, and exceptionally knowledgeable about the history of the region.[4]

3.2 Use a colon before a final clause, phrase, or word that explains, amplifies, or summarizes the preceding expression.

The colon here functions exactly as it does in 3.1: it alerts the reader that you're going to say more about the previous thought. The distinction here is that only one of the constructions is an independent clause.

> Honesty, integrity, and industriousness: these are what we value above all.

> Their "definitive" answer can be summarized in one word: *maybe*.

3.3 When you use a colon to introduce a list, make sure to write a complete thought first.

In other words, rather than write something like *Next year we must increase our marketing in: the West, the Pacific Northwest, and the Southern regions,*[5] it is much better to use no punctuation at all. Your lead-in should be a complete thought, as in *Next year, we must increase our marketing in three regions: the West, the Pacific Northwest, and the South.* Notice how the complete sentence does a much better job of helping the reader anticipate how the expression will end:

> Today we will discuss two topics: executive compensation and shareholder rights.

> She visited four countries: Portugal, Spain, France, and Italy.

> We have only three options: reduce the bid, increase the scope of work, or abandon the proposal.

3.4 Use a colon to introduce a vertical list when the list consists of sentence fragments.

When you break a sentence into a vertical list of ideas, it's best to write a complete thought as a lead-in. When you do, use a colon after the lead-in sentence.[6]

original:	To assist us in the planning process, please let me know your availability to attend, your interest in participating as a speaker, panelist, or poster presenter, and any topics or themes you would like to suggest.
revision:	To assist us in planning the event, please let me know the following:

- your availability to attend

- your interest in participating as a speaker, panelist, or poster presenter

- any topics or themes you would like to suggest

3.5 Use a colon to express direct ratio.

Note that direct ratio is always expressed in numerals.[7]

a ratio of 50:1

a ratio of approximately 3:2

5:4 odds

3.6 The colon is often used after the salutation line in correspondence.

After *Dear Ms. Rodriguez or Dear Dr. Matumbo*, use either a colon or a comma. Organizations that mandate one or the other usually mandate the colon. The comma is generally considered to be more personal, but we have to wonder how much attention the reader pays to the mark that follows the expression of endearment. People in love use commas, that's true. But the reader of workplace writing understands that the salutation is nothing more than a rubber-stamp formality, and she doesn't scrutinize the mark that follows in hopes of finding a subtle signal of your feelings about her.

3.7 Don't put a colon after a verb.

It's senseless to write something like *We need to track: our indirect costs, our direct costs, and our overhead costs more diligently.* A lot of writers do this, and I've never understood why. No colon should ever follow a verb. Rather than write, *The agent reported: terrorist activity is imminent*, the practical writer decides how much emphasis each idea should receive, puts the right words in the right order, and casts the expression so that it reflects his intent.

a single sentence, combining the two ideas:	The agent reported that terrorist activity is imminent.
subordinating the agent and emphasizing the terrorist activity:	According to the agent, terrorist activity is imminent.

3.8 In text, skip two spaces after the colon.

Skipping two spaces after the colon used to be routine. These days, many writers skip one space after the mark. This is not a good idea. In cases of summary statements and lists, we want our reader to see, instantly, what we're intending to do. The extra space helps ensure that she gets a good look at the mark, and this fosters comprehension.[8]

4. Comma

The use of the comma is logical, systematic, and consistent. The mark's main job is to separate ideas that the reader would otherwise mistakenly connect; its secondary job (never necessary in workplace writing) is to indicate the omission of a word or phrase.

4.1 Use a comma to separate two words or numbers that the reader might mistakenly connect on the first reading.

You must be able to recognize the potential for confusion in the following examples. Vigilance, empathy, and judgment are required.

Of the total, overtime was the greatest single direct cost.

To his older brother, Carl remained a complete mystery.

On August 13, 16 civilians were killed by a suicide bomber.

4.2 Use a comma to separate two or more adjectives when (1) the adjectives precede the noun and (2) you could substitute *and* for the comma.

crisp, vigorous writing

complex, time-consuming effort

calm, poised, collected demeanor

> **Sometimes the comma is unnecessary even if you could substitute *and* for it.**
> There's a big difference between coordinating adjectives and cumulative adjectives. I separate adjectives with a comma in *cold, windy day* but not in *little old lady*, even though the lady is both little and old. In that construction, *little* describes the phrase *old lady*.[9]

4.3 Omit the comma between cumulative adjectives.

We omit the comma in a phrase like *seven strange green flying objects*. In that construction, each adjective further builds a phrase. In other words, *flying* describes *objects*, *green* describes *flying objects*, *strange* describes *green flying objects*, and *seven* modifies the entire phrase *strange green flying objects*. When description accumulates like this, the adjectives are called "cumulative." No commas should separate them.

We also omit the comma when we use phrases that readers understand to be units, like *atomic energy*, *federal budget*, and *campaign contributions* in the following examples.

atomic energy program

federal budget deficit

illegal campaign contributions

4.4 Use commas to make plain that a word, phrase, or clause is parenthetical (not essential to the intended meaning of the sentence).

He has only one father:	His father, Leo, won the Nobel Prize in Economics.
There was only one foreman:	The foreman, Hank Gethers, rescued the injured worker.
if she has only one sister:	Her sister, Moira, has always been fiercely competitive.
There is only one Senate Ethics Committee:	The Senate Ethics Committee, which convened last night, voted to eliminate the provision.
a single-pilot aircraft:	The pilot, who bailed out over Turkey, has been rescued.
if we have received only one report	The report, received this morning, is alarming.
"much to his astonishment" could be cut:	The botanist, much to his astonishment, found himself falling in love with a specimen.

4.5 Don't use commas around any words that are essential to your meaning.

if the aircraft had two or more pilots:	The pilot who bailed out over Turkey has been rescued.
if we have received at least one other report:	The report received this morning is alarming.

> *if she has more than one sister:*   Her sister Moira has always been
> fiercely competitive.

4.6 Use commas to set off contrasting elements.

You could also use parentheses or dashes to set off these non-essential phrases.

> The French, not the British, designed the Concorde.
>
> The finished document, not the draft, is what matters most.
>
> What matters most is the finished document, not the draft.

4.7 Use commas to set off interrogative tags.

An "interrogative tag" is a little question tossed into the sentence, either in the middle or at the end. It's always parenthetical and always takes a pair of commas. Note that such a sentence ends with a question mark.

> We can still assume, can't we, that revenue will increase?
>
> The article was informative, wasn't it?

4.8 Use commas to separate items in a list that ends with **and or or.**

When you write *The contractor designed, built, and tested the device,* that comma after *built* is called "the serial comma." I encourage you to use this comma consistently.[10]

> Each analyst will research, prepare, and present a technical briefing.
>
> Complete forms 1099, 5500EZ, and 1806.
>
> We will be represented by Alice Kirk, Joan Schmidt, or Valerie Wharton.

If one or more of the items in the list requires internal commas, then commas won't suffice to separate them.[11]

4.9 Use a comma when you connect two independent clauses with and, but, or, so, or yet. Put the comma before the conjunction.

> We reviewed the analysis this morning, and Captain Gorday forwarded it to EUCOM.

> I read the report carefully, but the conclusions didn't make sense.

> Cease the hostilities immediately, or we will authorize NATO troops to intervene.

> The work has been completed, so we can invoice the client now.

> He says he hates to commute, yet he bought a house 50 miles from his office.

Note

Some authorities say you can break this rule when both independent clauses are short. If their only concern is brute readability, they have a point. *The evidence is convincing and we should act on it* is instantly clear, as is *The species is recovering but it remains endangered.*

In such sentences, omitting the comma may seem like a small matter, but you should write this way only when you intend to minimize emphasis on both thoughts. *Radar detected the flying object but the military never issued an alert.* There, both independent clauses are arguably short. But the comma is a rumble strip, and using it warns your reader to slow down and pay attention: *Radar detected the flying object, but the military never issued an alert.* If you wish him to pull over, stop the car, get out, and take some photographs, write *Radar detected the flying object. However, the military never issued an alert.*

4.10 Don't use a comma before a conjunction when you have one subject and two verbs.

In the pairs of examples that follow, the first construction consists of two independent clauses connected with a coordinating conjunction, and the comma is required. The second construction consists of one subject and two verbs (it makes no difference whether the verbs are active or passive). Note the difference in punctuation.

Mr. Tubbs flew to the site, and he inspected the damage to the reactor.

Mr. Tubbs flew to the site and inspected the damage to the reactor.

The prosecutor's arguments were eloquent, but they failed to convince the jury.

The prosecutor's arguments were eloquent but failed to convince the jury.

The drug has passed Phase II trials, and it is now awaiting FDA approval.

The drug has passed Phase II trials and is now awaiting FDA approval.

4.10.1 Break this rule when clarity demands it.

Disregard this rule when it provokes the absurd, as in the example below.

The congressmen ate and cursed the lobbyist.

Sure, context and common sense may make intention plain in that example. But I guarantee you that some readers are going to laugh out loud at the accidental picture of cursing congressmen cannibalizing a lobbyist. In a case like this, a decent writer would break the rule and add a comma to help make her meaning clear.

The congressmen ate, and cursed the lobbyist.

But a better writer wouldn't write that sentence in the first place. Remember Principle 1. The words come first. Use words and word order to structure your meaning; use punctuation only when you must.

The congressmen cursed the lobbyist as they ate.

Throughout their meal, the lawmakers cursed the lobbyist.

4.11 Always use a comma when your sentence consists of a dependent clause followed by an independent clause. Put the comma after the dependent clause.

Because the hard drive was damaged, we could not retrieve the data.

After we receive the go-ahead, we will begin the final phase of the project.

If the operation is successful, the patient should fully recover.

4.12 Don't use a comma when your sentence consists of an independent clause followed by a dependent clause.

no comma after "project":	We will begin the final phase of the project as soon as we receive the go-ahead.
no comma after "fail":	The advertising will fail unless we make it simpler.
no comma after "busy":	Everyone pretends to be busy whenever the CEO shows up.

Note

There's one exception to this rule, and it involves "extreme contrast." In *They continued to work on the project, even though funding had been cut off*, the dependent clause beginning with *even though* sets up a sharp contrast to what's said in the beginning of the sentence. Although a comma is not required here for clarity, using one strengthens contrast.[12]

4.13 Use a comma when your sentence begins with a phrase modifying the subject.

To her noses have always seemed unnecessary is a fairly strange thing to hear. When we punctuate it correctly, the idea may still seem strange, but at least it's clearly so: *To her, noses have always seemed unnecessary.*

Howling at the moon, the wolves epitomized the wilderness.

While conducting the research, she discovered that Ornstein's theory was flawed.

To begin with, Harris has never been willing to compromise.[13]

4.14 You can omit the comma after an opening word or phrase when clarity does not require it.

This is frequently true of transitions, as in the examples below.

Accordingly we find that the company has acted in good faith.

Next year they will introduce a 2-inch, high-definition disc.

In fact we clearly stated that the deadline had been changed.

4.15 Don't use a comma when you begin a sentence with a short phrase and the next word is a verb.

This construction is rare in business writing.

On the desk lay the half-finished report.

At the rear of Level 3 is the elevator.

Hidden behind the portrait was the safe.

4.16 When your sentence begins with a short indication of time, use judgment.

In the examples below, putting a comma after *1989* and *June* would not be wrong, but because a comma would not improve clarity here, all it would do is slow things down. Efficient design contains no unnecessary parts.

In 1989 the Cold War ended.

By June we expect to finish the project.

4.17 Use a comma when your sentence begins with an indication of time and the next word is capitalized.

Imagine the examples below without commas and you'll see why the mark helps here.

> In 1997, Lockheed Martin merged with Northrop Grumman.

> By April, Smith was nearly done.

> On May 30, ATMs malfunctioned at several hundred locations.

4.18 Convention requires that you use a comma after the date when you indicate both month and day.

> On October 23, she announced her resignation.

> On February 29, the protesters were arrested.

4.19 When you state a precise date (month, day, and year), always use a comma to separate day and year.

If the sentence continues, as in the second example below, put a comma after the year.

> The world changed on September 11, 2001.

> On July 6, 2009, she received the news.

4.20 In the "European" style used by military and intelligence writers, no comma is required unless it aids clarity.

> On 23 March 2009 the tanks were rolling toward Kazakhstan.

> By 1 December 2010 all agents must be proficient in the technology.

but

> On 17 August, Mancuso briefed the DI.

> On 9 June 2011, 64 confirmed sightings were reported.

4.21 *Put a comma after the clarifying devices* **i.e.** *and* **e.g.**

The device *i.e.* means "that is" or "in other words"; *e.g.* means "for example." By convention, both are placed inside parentheses. Be aware that readers often confuse these devices. A sensible option is to use the phrases *that is* and *for example* rather than the abbreviations.

> Some endangered species (e.g., the red wolf and the snowy owl) are being introduced into the park.

> The problems on *Mir* cannot be attributed to shoddy technology alone (i.e., human error has played a large role).

We occasionally see *e.g.* and *i.e.* preceded by a semicolon, as in *Please bring the important documents to next week's meeting; e.g., bring the deposition, the affidavit, and the original complaint.* Regardless of whether this usage is "correct," it is bad writing. It's bad writing because (1) the reader does not need a repetition of *bring* and (2) when you use an *e.g.*, you should immediately give examples of the *previous word*, not merely of some previously mentioned word. *We need to make copies of the important documents (e.g., the deposition, the affidavit, and the original complaint).* Precisely the same is true of *i.e.* The construction is added only as a clarifying device and does not deserve the status of a separate clause.

4.22 *Put a comma before* **etc.**

When the sentence continues, put another one after *etc.* When the sentence ends with *etc.*, the period after the abbreviation also serves to end the sentence.

> Hardware (computers, monitors, servers, etc.) is becoming less and less expensive.

> Please bring the contract, the amendment, the scope of work, etc., to the meeting.

> OGC is reviewing the contract, the amendment, the scope of work, etc.

4.23 Use a comma to separate elements of place names.

Their office is located in Potomac, Maryland, a suburb of
Washington, D.C.

Last year he was transferred to Stuttgart, Germany.

4.24 Use a comma to separate the elements in people's titles when you omit prepositions.

with prepositions:	She is Acting Head of the Personnel Division in the Bureau of Reclamation.
without prepositions:	Her official title is Acting Head, Personnel Division, Bureau of Reclamation.

4.25 Use a comma when necessary to separate digits in precise numbers.

Note that when you round a number, you use a decimal.

2,009	6.22 million (*rounded*)
9,717	6.2 million (*rounded*)
215,104	6 million (*rounded*)
6,218,639	

4.26 Use a comma to indicate you've omitted a word or phrase in a parallel construction.

Note the use of semicolons in this construction.

twice omitting "she transferred":	In January she transferred to Payroll; in June, to Accounting; in October, to Human Resources.
twice omitting "they have":	In California they have three offices; in Maryland, two; in Florida, one.

> **Stop**
>
> Let's agree right now that your reader prefers less complicated presentations of these simple ideas. In the workplace, it would be much better to write *She transferred to Payroll in April, to Accounting in June, and to Human Resources in October. They have three offices in California, two in Maryland, and one in Florida.*

4.27 Use commas to set off Jr., Inc., Ltd., and so on.

Follow the subject's preference here. A corporation may prefer *Tiger Industries Inc.* or *Tiger Industries, Inc.* Note that *Jr.* and *Sr.* are typically preceded by commas, but that *II, III*, and so on usually aren't.

> The meeting was facilitated by Harold Horn, Jr.
>
> The meeting was disrupted by Harold Horn III.
>
> Harold Horn, Esq., lives in Paris, Texas.
>
> Harry Horn manages Griffon, Inc.

4.28 Use the comma to set off "direct address."

Compare the meanings of *She knows how to shoot Tom* and *She knows how to shoot, Tom.* When you're writing to a single person and you use that person's name in a sentence, you're practicing what's called "direct address." Use commas to set off the name.

> We appreciate your suggestion, Ms. Malone.
>
> Ms. Malone, we appreciate your suggestion, and we will pass it on to the Executive Committee.
>
> We appreciate your suggestion, Ms. Malone, and we will pass it on to the Executive Committee.

The same principle applies if you're addressing a group. You'd write, *To summarize, my friends* rather than *To summarize my friends.* You'd write *We need to consider, ladies, how best to put the donations to work* rather than *We need to consider ladies.*

4.29 Use the comma to set off words or numbers in "apposition."

Appositives are usually short, and often they are parenthetical. When your primary meaning does not require them, punctuate them. All of the appositives in the examples below are non-restrictive, so they must be set off.

"Leila" is an appositive:	My wife, Leila, is a patent examiner.
"41–13" is an appositive:	The Redskins won, 41–13, in their best offensive game of the season.
"a consultant from GBT" is an appositive:	Krakatoa Jones, a consultant from GBT, has a quick temper.

4.30 Do not punctuate, with commas or anything else, when the appositives are necessary for your meaning.

In the examples below, the appositives aren't parenthetical—that is, you can't cut them from the sentence and still say what you mean—and so you do not punctuate them. Below, *Beatrice, Dizzy,* and *HOX-42* are restrictive appositives.

if she has more than one sister:	Her sister Beatrice likes jazz.
if he's written more than one book:	His book *Dizzy* is a best-seller.
since there are many different genes:	The gene HOX-42 contributes to a sense of despair.

4.31 Put the comma inside closing quotation marks.

This is the rule in American English. In British, Canadian, and Australian English, the comma always goes outside quotation marks. In legal writing everywhere, the comma goes wherever the attorney feels like putting it. Here is what convention says to do:

> "When I analyzed the data," she said, "I came to a different conclusion."

> "Layoff," "downsize," and "reduction in force" are euphemisms for firing people.

> His performance was rated "excellent," but he knew he could have done a better job.[14]

4.32 Use a comma to separate an introductory attributive phrase from a direct quotation.

In the examples below, the introductory phrases let the reader know exactly where the quotation came from. This is called "attribution."

> Mr. Greenspan quipped, "If what I've said is clear to you, then you have not understood me."

> The article concluded, "Warfare will never be the same."

> The advisor replied, "Mr. President, sometimes the facts lack actual factuality."

4.33 When you interrupt quoted material with an attribution, use commas as indicated below.

> "Exactly when," the shareholder asked, "are we going to see increased revenue?"

> "I used to think," the customer wrote, "that you cared about the environment."

"Writing in plain language," he said, "is the way we should've been writing all along."

4.34 When the attribution follows the quotation, punctuate as indicated below.

Note that you use a comma only when you quote a declarative sentence.

"It's time we looked into this matter," the executive said.

"What do you expect me to do with all this data?" Dr. Wells asked.

"Get your feet off my desk!" the CEO shouted.

4.35 Don't use a comma to introduce a paraphrase.

In the pairs of examples below, the first sentence requires a comma because we are quoting exact words and attributing those words to someone. The second sentence paraphrases the person's words, and those words should not be introduced with commas.

comma because of attribution:	He asked, "Has the meeting been postponed?"
no comma after "asked":	He asked whether the meeting had been postponed.
comma because of attribution:	She said, "I'll take care of it myself."
no comma after "said":	She said she'd take care of it herself.
comma because of attribution:	He wrote, "I don't understand the distinction."
no comma after "wrote":	He wrote that he didn't understand the distinction.

4.36 Put a comma after and, or, but, yet, or so when the words that follow are parenthetical.

We always set off parenthetical ideas, regardless of where they appear in the sentence. In the examples below, *waving to the audience* and *at least right now* could be cut. You could also use parentheses or dashes around such phrases.

> She walked toward the podium and, waving to the audience, tripped on the cable.

> The software has promise but, at least right now, does not suit our purposes.

4.37 Put a comma after First, Second, Next, Finally, and so on when you use these terms as transitions at the beginning of a sentence.

Here's how to do it:

> Bidding on this contract is a bad idea for several reasons. First, we have very little chance of winning it because the work is outside our area of expertise. Second, writing the proposal would require at least 200 hours of staff time, and we are struggling to meet the deadlines we already have. Third, the Statement of Work clearly indicates that Top Secret clearances are required, and only 4 of the 10 employees who would need to work on the project have that level of clearance. Let's not waste time pursuing an opportunity that isn't there.

4.38 Use a comma whenever you must to clarify your intent.

> God rest ye merry, gentlemen.

> God rest ye, merry gentlemen.

> They are protesting the award too aggressively.

> They are protesting the award too, aggressively.

Better:

They too are aggressively protesting the award.

5. Dash —

THE DASH EMPHASIZES THINGS.

Because of its width, the dash does the best job of moving ideas apart. It visually isolates a word or phrase. Thus it signals the eye that something worth noting is about to be said. In business and technical writing, we use dashes for three reasons: to surround non-essential material, to indicate how ideas relate, and to set up a summary statement.

5.1 Use dashes (instead of commas or parentheses) when you wish to emphasize parenthetical material.

If I write, *The new product, which took four years to complete, will be test-marketed in Charlotte next month*, my sentence is "correct." Commas are certainly correct there. And they would be appropriate if I wanted merely to indicate, with no particular emphasis, how many years the product took to be completed. But if I wish to stress that idea, then I use dashes instead of commas. *The new product—which took four years to complete—will be test-marketed in Charlotte next month.*

How much emphasis should the parenthetical idea receive? You're the writer; you're the only one who knows. You have three options—and if you remember that the reader reads whatever you put on the page, you'll choose the option that best conveys your intention.

no particular emphasis:	The President, reversing his position, now opposes the legislation.
weak emphasis:	The President (reversing his position) now opposes the legislation.

strong emphasis: The President—reversing his position—
                    now opposes the legislation.

5.2 Always use dashes around a parenthetical expression that strongly interrupts the flow of thought.

If you choose to appeal—the decision is up to you—you must notify us within 30 days.

We still have not heard from them—their response was due yesterday— regarding how they intend to resolve the dispute.

The Board of Directors decided—it was a vote that shocked shareholders— to eliminate the quarterly dividend.

5.3 Use dashes instead of commas whenever necessary to prevent misreading.

In the example below, the use of commas (while "correct") fails to indicate my intent.

In the writing we do at work, we should strive to be clear, to convey the meaning we intend, and we want the reader to understand the sentence the first time he reads it.

With commas, the sentence looks at first like a list. In fact, I want *to convey the meaning we intend* to define the word *clear*. Dashes do the job.

In the writing we do at work, we should strive to be clear—to convey the meaning we intend—and we want the reader to understand the sentence the first time he reads it.

In the first of the next two sentences, commas again disguise the intended meaning. A pair of dashes instantly indicates how the ideas truly relate. (Parentheses would work here too.)

The median sales price for all existing homes, single-family houses, townhouses and condominiums, was $212,800 in February, down 1.3 percent from a year ago.

The median sales price for all existing homes—single-family houses, townhouses and condominiums—was $212,800 in February, down 1.3 percent from a year ago.

5.4 You can use a dash (instead of a colon) to introduce a summary statement.

Use the dash for this purpose only when you want to *strongly* emphasize the concluding thought.

He remarked that there is only one important fact about humanity—at heart, people are and will remain superstitious savages.

The project manager came right to the point—productivity must improve.

5.5 You can use a dash (instead of a comma) before a coordinating conjunction between two sentences.

Again, do this only when you want to strongly emphasize the concluding thought. Here's what the usage looks like:

The audit revealed a major risk—and until that risk is resolved, we will not purchase any more of the company's bonds.

The policy was perfectly adequate when it was written—but that was 25 years ago, and the realities of the workplace have changed.

This use of the dash isn't mentioned in the grammar books, where a coordinating conjunction between two independent clauses must always be preceded by a comma. I wouldn't be surprised if some experts declare it to be overly dramatic or even "incorrect"—but your reader certainly won't. The dash, here, creates a rupture in flow more severe than that of the comma but not as severe as that of the period. In your writing, you are going to encounter times when your intended emphasis requires this usage.

The mark you use depends on exactly how much emphasis you intend each of your ideas to have. Remember what the marks do: the comma is no more than a rumble strip; the period is a red light. The dash is a speed bump that means business. Here's how it works:

> You respect your reader's time when you minimize the need to punctuate, and to do that, you structure your thought in a way that doesn't require much punctuation.
>
> You respect your reader's time when you minimize the need to punctuate. And to do that, you structure your thought in a way that doesn't require much punctuation.
>
> You respect your reader's time when you minimize the need to punctuate—and to do that, you structure your thought in a way that doesn't require much punctuation.

In the first example, all of the thoughts are presented in one sentence. The reader races through them all. The second example, consisting of two sentences, signals the reader to stop and process one thought before going on to the next. The last example is closely aligned with the second in terms of what we're doing with emphasis. All of the thoughts are presented in one sentence, but the reader cannot race through the expression. Here, the dash leads to a summary statement, one that you want your reader to pay particular attention to. The only thing unusual about this summary statement is that it begins with *and* or *but*.[15]

A final word about this highly nuanced usage. I see it a lot in good writing, and I suspect that experts on punctuation neglect to mention it because it's subtle and difficult to explain in a single sentence. I freely admit that it creates a relaxed and conversational tone. Sometimes that's what we want.

> **Note**
> Your keyboard doesn't have a single key that gives you a dash. When you want a dash, type two hyphens in a row. (Most word-processing programs will then automatically fuse the hyphens into a dash.) Whether you should cram the dashes right beside the surrounding words–like this–or space them apart from the surrounding words – like this – is a matter of fierce debate. Just be consistent.

6. Ellipsis `. . .`

The ellipsis indicates you've omitted words within quoted material. In workplace writing, that's its only job.

Suppose an excited politician said, "The American public is smarter than my Aunt Millie's mule, and while you can fool that mule with the same trick ten times a day, the people can't be fooled for long." If you quote this, you may decide to cut some words from the sentence; if you do, use the ellipsis:

> The Senator said, "The American public . . . can't be fooled for long."

> The Senator said, "The American public is smarter than my Aunt Millie's mule, and . . . can't be fooled for long."

6.1 When you exclude a word or phrase from the middle of a quoted sentence, use an ellipsis of three spaced periods.

leaving out "to the flag of":	"I pledge allegiance . . . to the United States of America."
leaving out "one small step for man":	"This is . . . a giant leap for mankind."

6.2 *When you are quoting two successive sentences and leave out the ending of the first sentence, use an ellipsis of four spaced periods.*

The first period acts as the end of the first sentence, and so it should not be spaced away from the previous character.

the original quotation:	The industry spokesman said, "Gasoline prices have jumped 33 cents a gallon over the past month and are expected to climb still higher at least through July. We expect record prices at the pump this summer."
if you leave out the last words of the first sentence:	The industry spokesman said, "Gasoline prices have jumped 33 cents a gallon over the past month and are expected to climb still higher. . . . We expect record prices at the pump this summer."
the original quotation:	"China reported a trade surplus in February of $23.76 billion, a ninefold surge from the same period a year earlier and one of the highest monthly totals ever. It came as top government officials reaffirmed promises to take measures to reduce the widening gap."
if you leave out the last words of the first sentence:	"China reported a trade surplus in February of $23.76 billion, a ninefold surge from the same period a year earlier . . . . It came as top government officials reaffirmed promises to take measures to reduce the widening gap."

6.3 *When you quote only a word, phrase, or fragment, don't use an ellipsis.*

no ellipsis required:	She referred to the new procedure as ". . . tedious and counterproductive . . ."

do it like this:	She referred to the new procedure as "tedious and counterproductive."
no ellipsis required:	The astronaut said the view of Earth was ". . . humbling in the extreme."
do it like this:	The astronaut said the view of Earth was "humbling in the extreme."

6.4 Refrain from using the ellipsis for any other purpose.

In workplace writing, what we want is razor-sharp communication. We can't achieve that unless we stick to the standards. Use the ellipsis only to let the reader know you've omitted words from a quotation.

The mark has other uses in other sorts of writing. A playwright uses it in dialogue to indicate a vocal pause suggesting hesitation, confusion, uncertainty, fear, or the inability to find words:

Man: How old are you?

Woman: Well, I'm . . . I'm . . . you mean *now*?

In the world of advertising, novice copywriters use it to try to create breathless suspense, as in *You've been waiting for it . . . and here it is!* Bad writers everywhere use it to suggest that they could say a lot more, but choose not to, as in *We will see how the client reacts. . . . I wouldn't be surprised if they accept. . . .*

If you try to use the ellipsis in these ways when you write at work, you'll be using a secret code, because your readers won't know exactly what you intend the mark to do. In workplace writing, use it only to indicate you've omitted words from a quotation.

7. Hyphen   -

The hyphen connects elements to show the reader that those elements form a single unit. It can connect a prefix to a word (*pro-Darwin*, *anti-amnesty*) to form a different word. It can connect words to form a compound noun (the global *sell-off*, a state of *self-awareness*) or compound verb (The package was *x-rayed*. Please *double-space* the text). It can also be used to indicate a span of time, as in *He served as Director from 2005-2010*.[16]

If your organization has a style guide, please consult it on this issue. Bonds that have a rating of "AAA" are called *AAA-rated* bonds at Fannie Mae and *Triple-A-Rated* bonds at Freddie Mac. Both are correct (though Fannie's is better because it is simpler). The *Washington Post* hyphenates *re-enter* (as in *Older Americans are re-entering the workforce*), but the word has no hyphen at NASA (as in *Friction is enormous when the shuttle reenters the atmosphere*).

7.1 Use a hyphen to indicate your intended sense of a word.

resign (to quit)   refund (to give money back)

re-sign (to sign again)   re-fund (to fund again)

7.2 Use a hyphen to join prefixes to capitalized nouns unless the combined form has become conventional.

An up-to-date dictionary supplies guidance here.

anti-European   pre-Columbian   pro-American

transatlantic   antisemitic   subarctic

7.3 Use a hyphen when you spell fractions.

one-tenth of our time

three-quarters of the shareholders

a majority of two-thirds

7.4 Use a hyphen when you give a precise numerical measurement.

Note that the numeral and the measurement (but not the noun) are hyphenated.

a 100-watt bulb   200-meter race

5-ton load   12-inch-diameter pipe

7.5 Use a hyphen to indicate a season that straddles two calendar years.

Note that you do not repeat the century (e.g., below, the *18* and *20* are omitted after the hyphen).

The winter of 1883-84 was especially severe.

He averaged 21 points per game in the 2008-09 season.

7.6 Use the hyphen that means "up to and including" to designate a continuous period of two or more years.

Note that with this construction, you do repeat the century.

The presidency of George Bush (1988-1992) was good for the domestic economy.

In his tenure as CEO (1997-2009), the company's market value tripled.

7.7 Use a hyphen to form compound nouns.

The follow-up is scheduled on November 17.

They marveled at the technology's cost-effectiveness.

He had a run-in with the Turkish police and is now imprisoned in Istanbul.

7.8 Use a hyphen to indicate "suspended compounds."

In a suspended compound, the important element is omitted in all but the last term. Here are a few examples. Note the space after the hyphen in the first two examples, and the commas following the hyphens in the last example.

> The proposal indicates both pre- and post-completion costs.

> They invest only in mid- and small-cap stocks.

> The boards are available in 8-, 16-, and 32-foot lengths.

7.9 Use a hyphen to clarify "improvised usage."

Context may fail to clarify intent in such sentences as *We made one last minute change to the proposal* and *They have agreed to provide a large scale model.* The reader needs either a comma or a hyphen.

a change made at the last minute:	last-minute change
a final and minor change:	last, minute change
a model built on a large scale:	large-scale model
a large model built to scale:	large, scale model

In the first example, using *minute* to mean *minor* would be silly because of the standard association of *last minute* with deadlines. Better adjectives here would be *minor, tiny, little, small, subtle, negligible,* and *minuscule.*[17]

7.10 Don't hyphenate two-word compounds when the first word is an adverb ending in -ly.

> the bitterly contested decision

> a clearly written apology

> a strongly worded warning

The reason you don't hyphenate these is that the adverb describes the next word alone. When you write *wholly owned subsidiary*, *wholly* describes *owned*. Above, *bitterly* describes *contested*, and so on.

7.11 Don't hyphenate foreign phrases used as adjectives.

> pro forma ceremony
>
> laissez faire attitude
>
> ad hoc committee

More practical advice would be to write only in English.

7.12 When a phrase is familiar and the hyphen does not aid clarity, you can omit it.

In each of the examples below, it's safe to assume that readers recognize the first two words as a unit of thought.

> federal budget deficit   ground attack aircraft
>
> Social Security legislation   human rights violations

Compassion for the reader is in order here. Always remember that familiarity with terms differs from readership to readership. Phrases like *spread spectrum analysis* and *frequency hopping system* require no hyphen at FCC because they have become terms of art among communications engineers. If, however, you're writing to a non-expert audience, then you are encouraged to hyphenate *spread-spectrum* and *frequency-hopping*.

7.13 Nearly all authorities say you shouldn't hyphenate compound adjectives when the first word is comparative or superlative.[18]

Then they tell you that the exception is *FBI's Most-Wanted List*. Following are commonly used examples of compound adjectives they say you don't need to hyphenate.

most favored nation	more advantageous solution
worst possible outcome	less developed countries

7.14 Break this rule when your meaning requires it.

Compound adjectives that begin with comparatives or superlatives sometimes require a hyphen. In the sentence below, taken from the *New York Times*, notice how *lower-ranking* is handled.

> The only other figure from the Bush White House to have been convicted of a serious crime is Donald McGonegal, a lower-ranking official who has been sentenced to 18 months in connection with the Jack Abramoff lobbying scandal.

There, *lower* is comparative, but we are not talking about an official who is both *lower* and *ranking*. We are talking about an official who has a relatively low rank. And even though readers would probably get this meaning, the hyphen enables them to get it a little more quickly.

The word *best* is superlative, but consider the difference in the following expressions:

> This is the best dressed salmon I've ever tasted.

> She was the best-dressed executive at the conference.

In the first example, *best dressed* does not take a hyphen because *dressed salmon* is the unit of thought. We are not applauding the salmon's choice of attire, but simply describing something called *dressed salmon*. In the second example, though, our unit of thought is not *dressed executive*. Instead we are describing an executive, and we are not saying that she is both the best executive and a dressed executive. Every organization I've ever been to requires employees at all levels to wear clothing. *Best dressed* is the unit of thought this time, and you indicate that by hyphenating it.

> Which member of Congress has received the most expensive gifts from lobbyists?

That sentence has two potential meanings, and that's always one meaning too many. We cannot know whether the writer intends *most expensive* as the unit, or whether he is talking about the greatest number of *expensive gifts*. If you intend the former, use the hyphen.

> Which member of Congress has received the most-expensive gifts from lobbyists?

7.15 It's better to use a hyphen when the rules say you shouldn't than to omit one when the reader needs it.

Your readers don't care about the rules of hyphenation. They care about clarity. I encourage you to hyphenate whenever doing so helps prevent ambiguity or facilitates understanding.

The compound adjectives below all begin with superlatives (which by rule aren't supposed to require a hyphen), but the reader benefits when you hyphenate. He benefits because he sees your intention *a little more quickly*. That is what we want.

> the best-case scenario   the best-kept secret
>
> the least-recognized fact   the worst-conceived plan
>
> the least-annoying error   the weirdest-rule award

7.16 Use the resources at your disposal.

Finally (it's worth repeating), always consult a current dictionary or your organization's style guide when you're unsure whether a particular compound is spelled as one word, is spelled as two words, or is hyphenated. Things change in a hurry. Today's word *email* took less than 15 years to evolve from *E-mail* through *e-mail* to its current form.

8. Parentheses ( )

Parentheses aren't used enough in today's workplace writing. Most people use them only to introduce an abbreviation, as in *She works for the Nuclear Regulatory Commission (NRC)*. That's conventional, but you should also develop the habit of using parentheses (1) to clarify how ideas relate, (2) to let the reader know that certain ideas have relatively minor importance, (3) to enumerate items in a list, as I'm doing here, and (4) to show exactly where lists begin and end. We'll cover those uses in this section.

8.1 Use parentheses to introduce acronyms and abbreviations (including unfamiliar abbreviations of measurement).

> He is being transferred to the European Command (EUCOM) next month.

> The Organization of Petroleum Exporting Countries (OPEC) cannot agree on a quota.

> We will introduce an Employee Stock Ownership Plan (ESOP) next year.

> Tachometers measure revolutions per minute (rpm).

> The maximum safe level of radon is 4 picocuries per liter (4 pc/l) of air.

8.2 Use parentheses to introduce formal and technical symbols.

> She decided to buy 500 shares of Duke Power (DUK).

> The "percent" symbol (%) must be confined to tables and graphs.

> After you have entered your password, press the "pound" key (#).

8.3 Use parentheses to enclose numbers indicating elements in a series.

> The screening committee rejected the proposal because (1) indirect costs are too high, (2) too few of the proposed personnel have security clearances, and (3) the company lacks relevant experience.

8.4 Use parentheses to enclose a word, phrase, or clause that you insert merely to clarify or explain something.

Such comments (called "asides") will then receive the right degree of attention from your reader. Note the placement of the periods in the last two examples below.

> Only one complainant (Bovarius) is willing to settle before trial.

> The German philosopher Gottlob Frege (1848–1925) laid the foundations of formal logic and of semantics.

> Herpetology (the study of reptiles) is fascinating.[19]

> The Pentagon is headquarters for the Department of Defense (previously called the War Department).

> The audit discovered three discrepancies. (All have since been corrected.)

8.5 Use parentheses to indicate you've added emphasis to a quotation.

If you italicize, underscore, boldface, or in any other way highlight quoted written text, indicate that you've done so at the end of the quotation. In the example below, note that *(italics added)* comes after the closing quotation marks and before the period.

> The engineer said, "With the new guidance system, we can launch from 10,000 miles away and strike within *three inches* of the target" (italics added).

Using *(italics added)* in that example is precise. Some writers prefer *(emphasis added)*. Make sure to use one or the other if you alter emphasis.

8.6 Use parentheses to assure the reader that you haven't added emphasis to quoted words.

Every now and then you'll quote some written text that contains boldface or italics. Suppose you are quoting a report's dramatic conclusion:

> "Under these circumstances, proceeding would be more than imprudent. **It would be preposterous**."

If you believe your reader may wonder whether *you've* boldfaced the last sentence—to bolster your argument or for any other reason—just do this:

> The report concludes, "Under these circumstances, proceeding would be more than imprudent. **It would be preposterous**" (emphasis in the original).

In the interests of being thorough, I want to add that brackets are sometimes used for the purposes in 8.5 and 8.6. The expressions *(emphasis added)* and *(emphasis in the original)* appear outside of the quotation marks, so readers should understand that these comments aren't part of the quotation. Thus it seems to me that *[emphasis added]* and *[emphasis in the original]* is an unnecessary use of distracting punctuation. But there is no consensus on this usage, so whether you use parentheses or brackets is a matter of preference. What's important, from the practical point of view, is that you let the reader know either that you've tinkered with emphasis or that the emphasis was in the original quotation.

8.7 Always use parentheses around i.e. and e.g. constructions.

> Illuminated manuscripts (e.g., *The Book of Kells*) are magnificent works of art.

All exempt employees (i.e., those who receive an annual salary) are expected to follow these procedures.

8.8 Use parentheses to enclose cross-references.

Income distribution remains uneven (see Table 2).

While making a comeback in some areas, the species remains endangered (see Figure 4).

8.9 Use parentheses to surround a parenthetical list that comes in the middle of a sentence.

We need to separate the items in the list with commas, but if we also use commas to surround the entire parenthetical expression, we get this:

We need more information about the applicant, including his clearances, the results of his previous polygraph tests, and whether he has ever visited Iran, before we can make a decision.

That may be correct, but it's not as readily grasped as this:

We need more information about the applicant (including his clearances, the results of his previous polygraph tests, and whether he has ever visited Iran) before we can make a decision.

8.10 Use parentheses to indicate that a non-essential expression has only minor importance.

This is where your judgment comes in. You're the writer. You're the only one who knows how much emphasis any idea deserves, and it's your responsibility to convey this nuance to your reader. Here's an example:

Most writers in the workplace, without thinking about the matter for an instant, would use commas in this sentence.

Most writers in the workplace (without thinking about the matter for an instant) would use commas in this sentence.

These days there's a decided knee-jerk reaction when it comes to punctuating non-essential expressions. People just toss a pair of commas in. Everyone agrees that commas are "correct" in the first example. In other words, commas are safe. But here's the thing: as your reader, I can't know your intention unless you put that intention on the page. If you want me to get the sense that *without thinking about the matter for an instant* is of minor importance, you must signal this to me, and the only way to signal it is to put the phrase in parentheses.

Although your reader never pauses to consider it, parentheses tell her, "I want you to save most of your attention for the rest of the sentence." Here are a few more examples.

The detective (a short, plump, disheveled little man with piercing eyes) questioned her for two hours.

Only two members of the jury (the others appeared half-asleep) laughed when the attorney asked the witness, "How many times have you committed suicide?"

The number of words in English (currently about 950,000, by most estimates) is increasing rapidly.

8.11 Parentheses are used to indicate alternative possibilities, but whenever you see them used that way, you're not seeing good writing.

What you're seeing is sloppy thought and terrible technique. This stuff appears only in the worst sort of boilerplate:

far too complex: The name(s) of the suspect(s) must be redacted.

Your pet(s) will be quarantined for six months.

Indicate the date(s) of your submission(s).

simpler, clearer, better: The name of each suspect must be redacted.

All pets will be quarantined for
six months.

Indicate the date of each submission.

You see this nonsense a lot (and especially) in legal writing. Here I have a boilerplate promissory note that begins as follows:

what it says: Maker(s) recognize(s) and acknowledge(s)
that Dealer retains a security interest in the
said vehicle up to and until such time as . . .

what it means: I agree that the Dealer owns the
vehicle until . . .[20]

8.12 Parentheses abuse readers when writers use them to repeat things that don't need repetition.

This happens in several ways, but most often with numbers. The examples below are absurd (but probably all too familiar).

We need to identify three (3) escape routes.

They received only 12 (twelve) responses to the RFP.

The Commission has received fourteen thousand two hundred seventy-one (14,271) complaints against the company.

As readers we encounter that sort of thing all the time. Many writers do it simply because they see it that way and think, "Well, I don't know why it's right, but I guess that's how it's done." I think it makes better sense to learn the rules pertaining to number use, and then follow the standards. Here's what your reader needs (anything more is excessive and distracting):

We need to identify three escape routes.

They received only 12 responses to the RFP.

The Commission has received 14,271 complaints against the company.

8.13 Use parentheses when commas don't suffice to clarify how your ideas relate.

For example, consider *Witnesses argued over whether the fistfight was started by Hugh Braley, the CEO, or the heckler*. On first reading, this list apparently consists of three possible instigators—but it could easily consist of two, with *the CEO* intended to describe *Hugh Braley*. Let's assume that the intended meaning is the latter. If all of your readers know that *Hugh Braley* and *the CEO* refer to the same person, commas suffice. But if some of your readers are unaware that *the CEO* merely describes Braley, they will see three instigators in that sentence. Here is where you need to use parentheses to clarify how the phrases relate: *Witnesses argued over whether the fistfight was started by Hugh Braley (the CEO) or the heckler*.

Your reader should not wonder—not for an instant—how ideas relate. In the examples below, assume that the second version expresses your intention. Parentheses take the guesswork out of such constructions.

I may have read three documents:	Yesterday I read Jackson's report, a 25-page analysis of our advertising, and the marketing summary.
I read two documents:	Yesterday I read Jackson's report (a 25-page analysis of our advertising) and the marketing summary.
The attorney may have three options:	Depending on his mood, the attorney drives an SUV, a GMC Yukon, or a 1968 Volkswagen Beetle convertible.

The attorney clearly has two options:

Depending on his mood, the attorney drives an SUV (a GMC Yukon) or a 1968 Volkswagen Beetle convertible.

Parentheses are often necessary to signal that a phrase is descriptive, not a separate item in a list. This is why you must pay no attention to those who insist that parentheses indicate carelessness, or that they are ugly, or that they are "informal," or for any other reason are best avoided.

PARENTHESES WITH OTHER PUNCTUATION

8.14 When a sentence begins in parentheses, put the period inside parentheses.

The analysis indicates a massive shift in consumers' buying habits. (They are beginning to put off buying big-ticket items.)

Artificial intelligence remains artificial. (Computers can't make intuitive leaps.)

8.15 When the expression inside parentheses ends a sentence, put the period outside parentheses.

Send your resume to Ms. Sharon Oliver (Chairperson, Selection Committee).

The species now proliferates in the Chesapeake Bay (and the Bay's larger tributaries).

8.16 Follow the standards when using parentheses along with commas, colons, dashes, and semicolons.

Here are a few examples.

commas in precisely the same positions as when we list "apples, bananas, and oranges":	Before you leave the room, make sure you (1) lock all classified documents in the safe, (2) shut down all computers, and (3) arm the security system.
commas after parentheses because the parentheses describe items in a list:	He visited Oxford (Pennsylvania), Cambridge (Maryland), and Paris (Virginia).
comma after parentheses because the parenthesis ends a dependent clause:	Since we last heard from her (three weeks ago), she has made amazing progress.
a semicolon after parentheses because another independent clause follows:[21]	The Redskins are 6–2 (their best start in five years); their schedule is tougher from now on.

9. Period

9.1 The period ends a declarative sentence.

That's its primary job. This is one of the few issues in punctuation that people don't squabble about. I'll bet that in any 1,000-word document, good writers use more periods than mediocre writers do. That's because good writers write shorter sentences.

The period ends the sentence, yes, but by isolating the thought it concentrates your reader's attention on that thought. It's perfectly correct to write *The committee has voted to begin impeachment proceedings against Senator Fitzvich; the Senator vehemently denies any abuse of power.* There's nothing wrong with that—but if you wish to emphasize each thought, you must give each one "sentence status," like this: *The committee has voted to begin impeachment proceedings against Senator Fitzvich. The Senator vehemently denies any abuse of power.* Short sentences punch the meaning home. Longer sentences, containing numerous ideas, dilute emphasis on each thought.

9.2 Put the period inside quotation marks.

This is simply a rule in American English. There are no exceptions. All newspapers and magazines published in this country follow it, and you should too. I can't help it if most lawyers either don't know this rule or ignore it. Where do your standards come from—from magazines like *Time* and *Newsweek,* or from promissory notes and mortgage agreements?

> The judge censured the attorney for prose he called "vague, verbose, and repetitive."

> The attorney replied, "Your Honor, I had temporary brain damage when I wrote this brief."

> The judge then ridiculed the attorney for claiming that the brain damage was "temporary."

> Members of the jury chuckled at what one of them later called a "vaudeville act."

9.3 There are differing rules for using the period with abbreviations.

The best advice here is to consult your organization's style guide. If your organization doesn't have a style guide, then pick one—pick the one your manager goes by—and follow its guidance.[22]

There are a number of conventions for using (or omitting) periods in abbreviations. These conventions often conflict.

The *New York Times* uses periods in *I.B.M., F.B.I., C.I.A.*, and so on. The *Washington Post* prefers *IBM, FBI,* and *CIA*. Whether it's better to use *U.S.* or *US* as an adjective (as in *U.S. troops*) is a matter of vigorous debate, as of course is whether it's best to use *U.S.A.* or *USA* as the noun (e.g., *This is her first visit to the U.S.A.*). Each camp finds the other's preference barbaric. The *AP Stylebook* insists there's no such abbreviation as *U.S.A.* or *USA*; it maintains that *United States* (never *United States of America*) is the noun. It does, however, concur with nearly everyone else that *U.S.* is okay, as long as it's used as an adjective. The *New York Times* blissfully ignores this advice from the AP and sprinkles *U.S.A.* (to stand for the country) throughout its copy. The *Washington Post* finds this to be absurd, insisting that *U.S.* is the abbreviation for the noun as well as for the adjective, arguing that context clarifies how the abbreviation must be understood. In its typical lackadaisical fashion, the *GPO Style Guide* agrees that *U.S.* (with periods) is the right way to abbreviate, but leaves open the question of whether *U.S.* is to be used as an adjective or a noun. The *Chicago Manual of Style* says *United States* should always be spelled out when used as a noun, with *U.S.* as the adjective form. But at this point, does it matter?

What all of this means is that sometimes you simply can't know whether your reader expects, for example, *UN* (without periods) or *U.N.* (with periods) as the abbreviated form of *United Nations*. A good writer always tries to minimize the burden on the reader, and a big part of doing so is to present ideas in expected, customary ways. But when conventions are in dispute, we can't satisfy everyone's expectations—and in such a circumstance, what matters most is being consistent within a particular document. Here I discuss those abbreviations where there seems to be a consensus on usage.

9.4 The abbreviations of most units of measurement do not take a period.

The notable exception is the abbreviation of *inch* and *inches*, which must be written *in.* to prevent momentary confusion. The examples below are both singular and plural.

ft	lb	oz	dwt	mph	yd	qt	gal	tbsp
	doz	rpm	cm	mg	km			

Let's not debate the matter. If you simply must put a period after *ft*, then do so. If you must abbreviate *pounds* as *lbs.* to avoid an overwhelming sense of aesthetic failure—or because that's what your manager thinks is correct—then do so. In matters of this sort, consistency is always more important than rules. Besides, in nearly all of the writing you do at work, you use these abbreviations only when drafting a document (that is, they don't survive in the final version).

9.5 American usage calls for the period after abbreviations of address.

In British usage, the period is optional when the first and last letters of the word appear in the abbreviation, so when you're reading *The Economist* and see *Ms Fitt* and *Mr Cobb*, remember that you're seeing British usage. If you're writing to people in the United States, punctuate as in the examples below.

Ms.   Mrs.   Mr.   Dr.   Hon.   Fr.   Rev.   Prof.

Gen. Patton   Rep. McClure   Sen. Mathias   Messrs. Jones and Smith[23]

9.6 When an abbreviated title comes after a name, punctuate as indicated below.

Note that a comma precedes the abbreviation.

Dante Alighieri, Ph.D.   James Joyce, L.L.D.   Herman Melville, M.D.

Don't put the title both before and after the name, as in *Dr. Walter Strong, M.D.*

9.7 When you abbreviate United States (as an adjective), use periods.

Most authorities agree on *U.S.* as the preferred form of the adjective.

U.S. interests   U.S. diplomacy   U.S. forces

9.8 Abbreviations of states require periods if you're not using U.S. Postal Code abbreviations.

And you shouldn't be using the Post Office's shorthand unless you're writing an address line. In your text, use the "old style" abbreviations like these:

Bethesda, Md.	Palo Alto, Calif.
Salisbury, N.C.	Middlebury, Ver.

Postal Code abbreviations do not take periods: MD, CA, NC, VT.

9.9 Use periods after abbreviated Latin terms.

If the sentence ends with an abbreviation requiring a period (as with *etc.*), don't add another period.

    i.e.   e.g.   etc.   Q.E.D.   P.S.   R.I.P.   ibid.   id.   n.b.

Try to minimize your use of the more unusual Latin abbreviations. *P.S.* and *etc.* are familiar to everyone, but the others can cause confusion and delay. I do not mean to be imposing my preferences of style here; it's simply my experience that many readers stumble over the others. Articles for publication and formal legal documents must follow specific "citation" styles, yes, but it does not follow that *n.b.* is any clearer than *z.B.* would be for readers of a marketing report.[24] Your points come across more readily when you write them in English.

9.10 A few words about abbreviations and "formality."

Many people say (because someone once said it to them) that abbreviations of any sort make your writing informal. Such a remark doesn't get us anywhere; it merely opens the door to endless philosophical debate. And there is never a victor in a conflict about "formality" because definitions vary wildly. Some people insist that writing is formal when it avoids four usages: contractions, abbreviations, symbols, and slang. Others insist that writing remains formal even if it contains abbreviations and symbols, as long as those usages are conventional and expected. Then they argue about whether "%" is conventional. Still others declare that abbreviations are formal but symbols are informal, which means you'd be formal with *Para. 3* but informal with "¶." No one can win the dispute because it is based on preference and whim.

What we want is writing that fits the occasion and the readership—and whether it's "formal" or "informal" by any individual's definition should not be a concern. Our primary concern should be clarity; the next should be economy. I can write out the phrase *Federal Bureau of Investigation* each time I use it, or—since clarity is not harmed and economy is improved—I can write *F.B.I.* (as is the style of the *New York Times*) or *FBI* (the style of the *Washington Post*).

When the abbreviation is what we're used to, the spelled-out version can be puzzling. Many people who have never heard of the *Occupational Safety and Health Administration* have a good sense of what *OSHA* does. Isn't it true that *IBM* is more familiar to you than *International Business Machines Corporation*? Isn't it true that *NASA* makes sense to you more quickly than *National Aeronautics and Space Administration*? Formality is not the concern here. Clarity is.

Furthermore, in the writing we do every day, we use many abbreviations without a moment's thought: we conventionally use *a.m.* and *p.m.*, for example, and if someone actually wrote *six ante meridiem* or *four post meridiem*, we would have to ponder the meaning—and then we would wonder what was wrong with him. Most readers would stop and stare at *Anno Domini 325* (is that some street address in Rome?) but would instantly catch the intent of *A.D. 325*.

The requirements of tone and formality differ from document to document. In certain documents, *i.e.*, *e.g.*, and *etc.* are conventional; in others, these abbreviations would surprise the reader and call attention to themselves. Because documents vary in their conventions of style, "It's always best to avoid abbreviations" and "It's always best to abbreviate" are equally oversimplified. If I were you, I wouldn't get caught up in considerations of formality when I'm trying to decide whether to abbreviate. I encourage you to behave practically. Abbreviate when doing so would not distract, when the abbreviated form is what the reader is used to, and when the abbreviation would save the reader time.

10. Question Mark ?

The question mark ends the interrogative sentence.

When does the meeting begin?

When she writes "bimonthly," what does she mean?

10.1 A sentence must end with a question mark when any element within it asks a direct question.

If you write *We can assume that revenue will increase*, you have written a declarative sentence. You end it with a period. But consider *We can assume, can't we, that revenue will increase?* That little *can't we*, called an "interrogative tag," asks a direct question. It affects the entire expression, and the sentence has to end with a question mark.

10.2 Writers often make the mistake of putting question marks at the end of sentences that aren't truly questions.

Should we proceed? is a question. *I wonder whether we should proceed* is a statement. Don't write *I wonder whether we should proceed?* or *They questioned whether the data were accurate?* In those expressions, you are stating what the subject does, not asking a question.

10.3 Put the question mark inside quotation marks when the quoted material is a question.

Do this regardless of whether you introduce the quotation with a statement or a question.

Here we have a statement about a quoted question:	She asked, "Has the meeting been rescheduled?"
Here we have a question about a quoted question:	Didn't he ask, "How long will it take for you to complete this project?"

10.4 Put the question mark outside quotation marks when the overall sentence is a question but the quoted material isn't.

Did the customer actually say, "These instructions are too simple"?

Shouldn't we ask about the meaning of "gobbledygook"?

10.5 The rules of English allow you to put a question mark in the middle of a sentence, but in workplace writing this is a bad idea.

It's a bad idea for the simple reason that your readers are going to think it's an error. At a minimum, it will distract. Rather than write *When will Phase II be completed? is the next question*, it's better to rephrase: *Next, we would like to know when Phase II will be completed*.

11. Quotation Marks

11.1 Use quotation marks to indicate that someone else (not you) either said or wrote the exact words.

According to the mission specialist, the Mars landing is a "spectacular scientific achievement."

In his report, Blake states, "Demographic shifts are in our favor."

When asked why he did not take the shorter route, the truck driver replied, "I'm taking this route because this is the route I always take. I've taken this route all my life, and I'm not changing it!"

11.2 Use quotation marks to indicate that a particular word or phrase is intended ironically.

It actually complicated everyone's taxes:	the 1986 Tax "Simplification" Act
In fact, they were very dangerous places to be:	"safe" havens in Bosnia

11.3 Use quotation marks to introduce an unfamiliar or technical term.

> The robot's "end effectors" (i.e., hands) are almost as nimble as a human's.

> When the rate of growth slows, economists call the phenomenon "negative growth."

11.4 Use quotation marks to indicate that a word or phrase is to be seen as a term, rather than as an ordinary part of speech.

The phrase that comprises should be that includes makes no sense at all unless I show you how to understand the intent: *The phrase "that comprises" should be "that includes."*

> "You" means the loan applicant, and "it" refers to the lender.

> Barnes uses "proactive" far too often.

> BARF is derived from "Bureau Agenda Release Form."

11.5 Use quotation marks to set off the titles of poems and songs, and to set off a discrete section of a larger document.

The titles of larger works—books, magazines, journals, etc.—are italicized. Discrete sections of those works (titles of chapters of a book, titles of articles in a magazine, and so on) take quotation marks.

> In college she had to memorize Frost's poem "Stopping by Woods on a Snowy Evening."

> Chapter 3, "The Double Helix," is the most important chapter of her book, *Theory of Genetics*.

> In the December 4 issue of *Time*, there is a fascinating article entitled "Life in the Slow Lane."

> "On the Street Where You Live" is her favorite song from *West Side Story*.

11.6 Use "single" quotation marks only when you must quote something within a quotation. (The apostrophe serves this purpose.)

> The memo states, "Documents classified as 'Secret' or higher may not be reproduced except in secure areas."

> In the preface, the author writes, "The problem with the phrase 'functional illiteracy' is that it isn't functional—it's unclear."

11.7 For lengthy quotations, isolate and indent the text.

When the quotation occupies three or more lines of text, you can improve readability by visually isolating it. Skip a line and roughly center the words. When you format that way, don't use quotation marks, but remember to make the attribution plain with your lead-in sentence. I might wish, for example, to quote the infamous Professor Squeam, who had this to say about being abducted by aliens:

> Let me stress this: there was nothing compassionate in their actions. With all the disinterest of mechanics removing a piston, and without giving me anything to numb the pain, they sawed my skull in half, bared my brain, and pierced it with what looked like meat thermometers. That was decidedly unpleasant. I could see and feel everything the entire time because they hadn't severed the spinal cord. I appreciate their closing my skull and healing me before they returned me to my study, but to this day my scalp itches incessantly. That's how I know it truly happened.

It's always a good idea to show the reader, visually, that one section of your text differs in nature from another. This format is useful for longish quotations of all sorts: citations of rule, of policy, of chunks of correspondence, and so on.

QUOTATION MARKS WITH OTHER PUNCTUATION

11.8 The period always goes inside quotation marks.

This is simply the convention in the United States. There are no exceptions. Don't bother trying to figure out why.

> The engineer characterized the construction as "substandard and flimsy."

> "I think," she said mysteriously, "that you're in for a pleasant surprise."

> 35 U.S.C 103 states that patentability "shall not be negatived by the manner in which the invention was made."

11.9 What about when I'm quoting a Web address?

Internet addresses need to be precise, and for this reason some authorities say it's okay to put the period outside quotation marks when the quoted material ends with any form of URL, as in the example below.

> Please visit our website at "www.blasquasm.com".

I understand the intent, but to me that simply looks wrong. Worse than wrong—*British*. In point of fact, your browser disregards the period at the end of the Internet address. What this means, in practical terms, is that your reader can access a link, or cut and paste it, when the period is inside closing quotation marks, as in the following:

> You can reach me by email at "Jsmith@USJG.gov."

And you could avoid the issue entirely by putting the address in italics.

11.10 The comma always goes inside quotation marks.

This is (like the placement of the period) the convention in American usage. It's a rule. There are no exceptions.

> They call it a "wooden interdental stimulator," but it's really just a toothpick.

"The design is superb," the customer said.

"This program," the congressman grumbled, "is a disaster waiting to happen."

11.11 The colon, dash, and semicolon always go outside quotation marks.

This is not a rule, per se, but it may as well be one. Here's why. Chances are zero that you'll ever choose to quote someone and end the quotation where the person used (for example) a colon. That makes no sense at all. But you could easily decide to use the quotation as a lead-in to a list or summary statement, and in that case, using the colon would be your decision (and certainly not part of the original quotation). Precisely the same logic holds for the dash and for the semicolon.

Avoid "proactive": the word is used to mean a dozen different things.

The plural of "Dr." is "Drs."; the plural of "Mrs." is "Mmes."

"This species," the biologist said, "devours itself in captivity"—a phenomenon animal psychologists call "depressive auto-cannibalism."

11.12 The question mark goes inside quotation marks whenever the quoted material is a question.

When the overall sentence is a question, but the quoted material is simply a declarative statement, then the question mark goes outside the quotation marks (as in the last example here).

a statement about a question:	The auditor asked point blank, "Exactly when will we receive the finished report?"
a question about a question:	Did the client ask, "Will you itemize the charges on the invoice?"

a question about a statement:	Do the instructions say, "Attach the red wire to the positive and the black wire to the negative"?

11.13 Like the question mark, the exclamation point goes inside quotation marks whenever the quoted material is exclamatory.

When the overall sentence is exclamatory, but the quoted material is a declarative statement, place the exclamation point outside quotation marks (as in the last example).[25]

a statement about an exclamation:	The excited politician cried, "I'll vote any which way they want me to!"
an exclamation about an exclamation:	I hate it when I hear commercials blaring, "Breakfast is the most important meal of the day!"
an exclamation about a statement:	We can't let them get away with calling our product "cheap"!

11.14 When you quote an entire sentence and begin with an attribution, put a comma after the attribution.

Davis muttered, "Why am I always the last one to know?"

The report concludes, "Consolidation will certainly continue in the banking industry."

The psychiatrist said, "I'm afraid I can't see your invisible friend."

11.15 When you give the attribution at the end of the quotation, punctuate with a comma, question mark, or exclamation point, as appropriate.

"We have every reason to be optimistic," the attorney insisted.

"Can we expect increased earnings in the fourth quarter?" the CEO asked.

"Drat that Dark Lord!" Frodo groused.

11.16 When you interrupt a quotation with an attribution, punctuate with commas.

Note that two sets of quotation marks are used.

"My point," he said, "is that we could be much more productive."

"Why is it," the author asks, "that a broken heart leads to religion?"

"Your invisible friend," the psychiatrist gasped, "has *horns!*"

11.17 When you're quoting only a fragment or a phrase, don't put a comma before the quotation.

The press release states that a dividend increase "will certainly occur this year."

They termed the lawsuit "ridiculous and frivolous."

According to McLaren, the report "does not fully explain the situation."[26]

11.18 Use quotation marks after such words as named, entitled, termed, called, and so forth. Note that no comma follows these words.

At the inquest, his death was deemed "death by misadventure."

She was named "Most Likely to Look in the Mirror" by her classmates.

The report entitled "From Technology to Nanotechnology" offers a fascinating perspective.

11.19 Don't use quotation marks when introducing an abbreviation in parentheses.

Forty years ago, people took great pains to introduce an abbreviation, as in *Bureau of Land Management (hereinafter referred to as "BLM")* or *International Business Machines Corporation (referred to henceforth as "IBM")*. You still see it this way from time to time, but usually in legal writing. Let's keep it confined there.

Today's convention for introducing an abbreviation is much simpler. We no longer write anything like *hereinafter referred to as* (since readers know this without our help) and we no longer use quotation marks around the abbreviation. What you see below is what the reader needs—anything more would be excessive.

> Department of Justice (DOJ)
>
> National Heart, Lung, and Blood Institute (NHLBI)
>
> improvised explosive device (IED)
>
> President of the United States (POTUS)

12. Semicolon ;

Even the name of this thing is trouble. It should be called a "super-comma" or a "semiperiod" because its practical effect is to bring things to a near stop. But someone named it semi*colon*, and the name stuck, and there's not much we can do about it. In workplace writing, this misunderstood mark may be used in five ways. I say "may be used" and not "is used" or "should be used" because you often sacrifice clarity when you drop a semicolon into a sentence.

12.1 A semicolon may be used to connect independent clauses when there is no conjunction between them.

Generally speaking, the semicolon works best when the independent clauses are (1) relatively short, (2) parallel in structure, and (3) do not deserve the status of separate sentences. That last issue is yours to decide.

CXD employs 90,000 people; AFR employs 146,000.

Meriwether invented the device; Slovo received the patent.

Fannie Mae stock lost 8 percent last year; Freddie Mac stock gained 6 percent.

Be aware of the limited usefulness of this construction.
Here the semicolon has exactly the same meaning as ", and." The examples above are correct, but they do not tell the reader anything about how the thoughts relate. Don't settle for being correct. If you mean *Meriwether invented the device, but Slovo received the patent*, then say that. If you mean *Even though Fannie Mae stock lost 8 percent last year, Freddie Mac stock gained 6 percent*, then say that. Make your meaning plain with words.

12.2 A semicolon may be used to connect two independent clauses when the second independent clause is introduced by a transitional phrase.

Note that *a comma always follows* the transitional word or phrase.

The new procedure will save time and money; more to the point, it will increase safety.

A new CEO will be hired next year; in the interim, Smith will serve as chief executive.

The chain of custody was tainted; as a result, the judge threw out the evidence.

12.3 A semicolon may be used to connect two independent clauses when the second independent clause is introduced by what English teachers call a "conjunctive adverb."

Among the most commonly used conjunctive adverbs are *accordingly, consequently, furthermore, hence, however, indeed, moreover, nevertheless, nonetheless, otherwise, still, therefore,* and *thus.* Please note that a comma always follows these words when you use them as conjunctions.

> We cannot publish your novel at this time; nevertheless, we encourage you to keep writing.

> The method must be repeatable; otherwise, the results will be considered invalid.

> Our competitors are gaining market share; furthermore, they are expanding overseas.

12.4 Use a semicolon when you are listing ideas that are (1) closely related and (2) slightly complex.

In the two examples below (taken from a hypothetical newspaper), none of the items in the lists requires any internal punctuation, so commas could logically separate them. The writers, with good judgment, use semicolons instead.[27]

> All of the candidates for this year's Golden Jabberwock award hold named professorships at prestigious universities. Parker Johns is Nodanudder Professor of Ethics at Princeton; Elizabeth Auchinfee is H. Paul Fopa Professor of Linguistics at Harvard; Henri Belloq is J. J. Queasel Professor of Comparative Religion at Columbia; Roxana Olescu is Farrago Professor of Philosophy at Yale.

> Attacks by animals that are usually peaceful have been spreading throughout Washington, D.C. A pigeon assaulted a police officer in Georgetown; deer kicked out the windshields and side windows of several parked cars in McLean Gardens; a flock of seagulls pecked at the head and neck of a jogger near the Kennedy Center; a pair of squirrels harassed a

lobbyist in Foggy Bottom by climbing up inside the legs of his trousers and forcing him to whip off his pants in full view of hundreds.

In these examples, the writer does not wish to put each item in a separate sentence because *that would disguise how the items are related*—they comprise a list of thoughts pertaining to one topic. He does not wish to use commas, either, because doing so would coax you into speeding through the sentence. In other words, commas would not emphasize each idea enough. The semicolon provides more "stopping power" than the comma, but not as much as the period.

12.5 A semicolon may be used to separate items in a list when one or more of those items requires a comma of its own.

The first example below shows a reasonable use of this technique. Here, commas would not clearly separate each item because each one already contains a comma.

> Members of the panel include Frank Danziger, CEO of Fairborn; Lindsay Venstrom, President of Arquebus; Ray Grant, Deputy Director of the Department of Justice; and Zoe Kirchner, Professor of Ethics at Yale University.

Here's another (unedited) example. It embodies the same technique, but this time the technique results in something you probably don't want to read.

> The specific tasks involved will be: review and evaluate with ECIB all aspects of the online community toolset for tailoring to ECIB needs; establish a work plan for completing project by October 2010 including strategies to seed the community, supply user-valuable information and exchange opportunities, and seed the COLP library; produce working COLP with content manager that enables ECIB to make text, information, and image changes to the website at any time and remotely without use of programmers; ensure COLP supports NIH privacy and website policies for data collection, questionnaires, Section 508 access, .gov URL and federal website designations, does not use persistent cookies, and follows similar federal guidelines detailed in the Scope of Work document; ensure

the COLP includes ability to add new groups of members to the community website in the future, as detailed in the Scope of Work; ensure the COLP functions as a contract database for NHGRI to contact all members and groups of members by geographic location, grade level teaching, NHGRI courses attended, etc as described in the sow; ensure the COLP includes unrestricted use of the Healia search mechanism (Healia.com) and that the use of the engine is not subject to renewal fees or limited aspect of use by NHGRI; communicate with ECIB on a bi-weekly basis as to project status; provide for ECIB review of the website and for changes that are required and determined in the review phase; provide ability to generate website statistics on usage patterns, non-functioning pages, and similar review parameters which result from initial review of online toolset with ECIB; provide eight (8) hours of programmer time for maintenance and ECIB changes per month for the first year of operation.[28]

This is what we get from writers who know the rule about semicolons but don't use common sense. Whether punctuation is correct isn't the issue anymore: format is monstrous, and the outcome is unfair to the reader. When commas alone don't suffice to clearly separate the items in your list, semicolons may not be the best solution. You should try (1) grouping closely related items into separate, shorter lists; (2) using numbers in parentheses to introduce the items; or (3) formatting your list vertically, using bullets.

12.6 Try using numbers instead of semicolons.

When you use numbers in parentheses to separate the items in a list, you preserve the shape (the appearance) of a sentence. Maintaining "sentence shape" is important when the alternative—using bullets in a vertical list—would put too much emphasis on the ideas.

Here's an example of semicolon use from an application for a patent. The name of the invention is "Improved Interpersonal Pursuit Method." The inventor seeks to patent a method for a man's seducing a woman.[29]

> The method comprises instructing the male how to initiate attraction on the part of the female; establish female-to-male interest; establish a connection with the target female; establish comfort with the target female, which consists primarily of conversation; and promptly after conclusion of the step of establishing comfort, seduce the target female and have sexual intercourse with her.

Semicolons are used correctly there. But here's the same paragraph with numbers used instead. As a reader, which version do you prefer?

> The method comprises instructing the male how to (1) initiate attraction on the part of the female, (2) establish female-to-male interest, (3) establish a connection with the target female, (4) establish comfort with the target female, which consists primarily of conversation, and (5) promptly after conclusion of the step of establishing comfort, seduce the target female and have sexual intercourse with her.

Such phrasing as *target female* aside, do you find the second version easier to read? Most people do. The numbers function far more efficiently than semicolons in indicating, visually, where items begin and end. Another advantage of this technique is that your reader sees at a glance how many steps there are in the procedure. Note that when you use numbers to separate the items, you also use commas (nothing else).

12.7 Try using bullets in a vertical list instead of semicolons.

First of all, here's an example of the overly difficult sort of semicolon use we're trying to avoid. What results is a format with all the charm of a thicket of thorns:

> Highlights of next month's issue include "From Medieval Torture to Modern Dentistry," by Lemmy Yankemall (the Howling Dentist); "Fighting the Feeling of Futility," by Dr. Ugo Zumhölle; "Is It Really Fun to Take Pleasure in Others' Misery?" by Dr. Mi Sad Tu; and "Depression and Digestion: The Real Reason You're Constipated," by Dr. Donna Kant-Scatwell.

Using semicolons there may be "correct," but I'll bet you'd prefer to read this:

Next month's issue will include several thought-provoking articles:

- "From Medieval Torture to Modern Dentistry," by Lemmy Yankemall (the Howling Dentist)

- "Fighting the Feeling of Futility," by Dr. Ugo Zumhölle

- "Is It Really Fun to Take Pleasure in Others' Misery?" by Dr. Mi Sad Tu

- "Depression and Digestion: The Real Reason You're Constipated," by Dr. Donna Kant-Scatwell

For detailed guidance on how to punctuate the many varieties of lists, please see the appendix, "How to List Ideas."

13. Slash ╱

This mark has at least half a dozen other names, some of which sound heroic (*solidus, virgule,* and *separatrix* would be excellent names for Musketeers), but a practical writer calls it a slash, because *slash* is the simplest, most descriptive, and most common name for it. You can use it well in several ways. You can befuddle the reader with it in countless ways. The mark can imply *or, and, for, per,* combinations of these, and other relationships as well.

13.1 Use the slash to indicate per in highly technical abbreviations.

The density of gold is 19.32 g/cm^3.

The speed of sound at sea level is 340.29 m/sec.

13.2 Use the slash to indicate a 12-month period overlapping two calendar years.

budget year 2009/10

academic year 1998/99

the 2010/11 basketball season

13.3 Use the slash when its use has become conventional to indicate that two cities are to be seen as a unit.

Here the mark is understood to mean *and*. Note that in this construction it's conventional to put a space before and after the slash.

Tampa / St. Petersburg

Minneapolis / St. Paul

the Washington / Baltimore area

13.4 Use the slash when your audience expects it in common abbreviations.

Your judgment has to tell you whether the occasion calls for *price-to-earnings ratio* or whether *P/E* suffices. Specialized writing of all sorts makes frequent use of the slash, as in *r/w disc, i/o port,* and *TCP/IC.* We can regard these usages as jargon; as is true of all jargon, they provide efficient shortcuts when the audience understands them and expects them. More generalized writing also has common abbreviations that use the slash. *C/O* is more familiar than *in care of.* Writers of forms need to be careful with *N/A*, because readers sometimes need guidance on whether it is short for *not applicable* or *not available.* A brief explanation or footnote would help.

13.5 Use the slash in compounds when the relationship is intuitive.

Good examples of this usage are *work/life balance* and *love/hate relationship.* These are far more concise than *a balance between the demands of work and the enjoyment of life* and *a relationship that swings between the extremes of love and hate.* We can safely assume that our readers will get the meaning of *pass/fail.* In such constructions our intent is intuitive.

13.6 Beware of the slash used in **his/her, he/she, s/he, w/o,** and similar shorthand forms.

In workplace writing, many readers see signs of laziness in such abbreviations as *w/* for *with*, *w/o* for *without*, and *24/7* for *anytime*. Lots of readers also find *his/her, he/she, s/he,* and all variations on that theme to be distracting eyesores. If you can't find a way to avoid gender bias, it's best to spell out *his or hers*, or *hers and his* (depending on your politics), and to do the same with all alternative pairs.

13.7 It's best not to use the slash to separate month, date, and year.

Most people who know U.S. conventions would probably assume that *9/6/11* refers to September 6, 2011. But in the military, in some intelligence agencies, and throughout Europe, *9/6/11* is understood to refer to 9 June 2011. What this means is that if you abbreviate dates with slashes, you continually have to remind yourself of your reader's expectations about this minor matter of style. Considerations of formality aside, it simply makes more sense to spell out the date.

13.8 Use the slash in the construction **and/or** only after you've made sure you don't mean **and** or **or.**

Used sensibly, *and/or* has the meaning of *one or the other, or both*. In the example below, from a report on a clinical trial, some patients with arthritis took glucosamine, some took chondroitin, some took both, and some took a placebo. Because some took both and some took one or the other, *and/or* is logical.

> The dietary supplements glucosamine and/or chondroitin fared no better than the placebo in slowing the structural damage of knee osteoarthritis.

And/or is logical in these examples too:

Either (or both) could be causing the deforestation:	The deforestation may be caused by microscopic parasites and/or chemical pollution.

| *Either (or both) could have* | The crash was caused by mechanical |
| *caused the crash:* | failure and/or pilot error. |

Either (or both) could be the	The jump in earnings results from
reason for the jump in earnings:	increased advertising and/or increased
	prices.

But before you use *and/or*, make sure you don't mean something simpler—like *and* or *or*. The examples below make no sense if you think about them.

| *The right word is "or":* | Bring your passport and/or driver's |
| | license to the security desk. |

| *The right word is "or":* | The company and/or the union may |
| | choose arbitration. |

The right word is "and":	The maximum penalty for speeding in a
	construction zone is a $10,000 fine
	and/or six months in prison.

14. Punctuating Common Sentence Structures

The way a sentence is structured determines whether punctuation is required, though you frequently have to decide which mark best suggests your intent. Here are the common sentence structures and the appropriate ways to punctuate them. (If you've forgotten what dependent and independent clauses are, refer to the "Definitions" section.)

14.1 DC, IC: A Dependent Clause Followed by an Independent Clause

As soon as we receive the go-ahead, we'll get started on the project.

If you have any questions, please contact Ms. O'Rourke.

Until we install the barricades, we remain vulnerable.

Because the CEO could not attend, the meeting was postponed.

Note that you put a comma immediately after the dependent clause. A comma always goes there; nothing else ever does.

14.2 IC, DC: An Independent Clause Followed by a Dependent Clause

We will notify you after we make our selection.

Please contact Ms. O'Rourke if you have any questions.

Pay close attention to terms of art when you revise your report.

The plaintiff maintains that she wasn't informed until the deadline had passed.

No comma goes anywhere in these sentences (just the opposite of DC, IC).

Note

There are two important exceptions to this rule. The first occurs in the case of "extreme contrast." When your dependent clause begins with *though, although, even though*, or *even as*, you are setting up an outcome that contrasts to some degree with what you've said in the beginning of the sentence. If you wish to suggest sharp contrast, use a dash or a comma; if you wish to suggest only mild contrast, don't punctuate at all.

The examples below demonstrate how these contrast signals work.

Sharp contrast:

The Iraqi spokesman insisted that U.S. troops were nowhere near Baghdad, even as he winced from the nearby explosions.

She continues to maintain that she was driving 55 miles per hour—even though the trooper followed her at 80 miles per hour for more than two minutes.

He referred to the committee's decision as "callous and hateful," although he later claimed he said nothing of the sort.

Mild contrast:

They won the contract even though they lacked experience.

The evidence was admitted even though it was obtained illegally.

The second exception occurs when you use *because* between two sentences. This one requires a few words to explain.

14.2.1 IC because IC

When you write *She missed the flight because she was stuck in traffic,* you are explaining an event. Effect (missing the flight) and cause (traffic) are equally necessary to this purpose. Every word is essential to meaning. In other words, the clause that begins with *because* isn't parenthetical. It's simply a dependent clause, and no comma should precede it. *Laura never wears opals because she believes they bring bad luck* explains why Laura never wears opals. *Ludwig never eats eggplant because he hates the way it tastes* explains why Ludwig never orders moussaka.

Most of the time, this is what you're doing when you put *because* between two sentences. Each of the examples below explains a situation or event. Every word is necessary to that purpose, and no comma precedes *because.*

They won the account because they listened to the customer.

We rewrote the pamphlet because our focus groups couldn't understand the original version.

The species is being removed from the endangered list because its habitat has been restored.

14.2.2 IC, because IC

Put a comma before *because* when you state the reason for an inference or use *not* in the main verb.

INFERENCE

She ate all the doughnuts because she was starving explains an event. It explains why she ate all the doughnuts. *She must have been starving because she ate all the doughnuts* doesn't work that way. She wasn't starving because she ate doughnuts. Here, the *because* clause doesn't explain an event, but explains why you infer something. *She must have been starving, because she ate all the doughnuts* is what you should write.

The missile must have exploded because it disappeared from radar is not what you mean. Vanishing from a radar screen doesn't cause a missile to explode. *The missile must have exploded, because it disappeared from radar* is what you should write.

In the examples below, the writer states a reason for an inference. Just imagine the sentences without commas, and you'll see why the mark is necessary.

> They must have gone out of business, because I can't find them listed anywhere.

> He assumes you think you're overweight, because you drink Diet Coke.

> The attorney must be worried, because she looks as though she hasn't slept.

NEGATION

Clarity often suffers when a writer uses *not* as part of the main verb.

> Olaf was not found guilty because the jury understood the law.

That expression provokes some readers to wonder whether Olaf was found guilty for a different reason. Could he have been found guilty because the jurors feared him, or because they despised him, or because they were dazzled by the prosecutor? Context should clarify the matter, but that's no excuse to write a crippled construction. If you mean that he was found *not guilty*, say so. Take care to put *not* where it belongs.

> Olaf was found not guilty because the jury understood the law.

When you write it that way, no comma is required. If you leave *not* in the wrong place, you need to put a comma before *because*:

> Olaf was not found guilty, because the jury understood the law.

The comma shows the reader that the clause beginning with *because* is parenthetical. In other words, it shows her that the main point of the sentence is that Olaf was found not guilty. The same principles apply to the examples below. Assume that in each case the writer intends the first clause to be the main point.

Is it persuasive for a different reason?	The argument is not persuasive because it appeals to emotion.
If the argument is not persuasive, use a comma:	The argument is not persuasive, because it appeals to emotion.
The assertion requires no comma:	The argument is unpersuasive because it appeals to emotion.
Was he indicted for a different reason?	The lobbyist was not indicted because he refused to testify.
If he was not indicted, use a comma:	The lobbyist was not indicted, because he refused to testify.
The assertion requires no comma:	The lobbyist avoided indictment by refusing to testify.

14.3 S V and V: One Subject and Two Verbs

> We arrived at the site and inspected the damage.
>
> The EVP glanced at the executive summary and howled in dismay.
>
> We need to listen to our customers and simplify the policy.
>
> The animal has escaped and is loose somewhere in the lab.
>
> The agency monitors and regulates toxic waste sites.

Note that there is *no punctuation* when (1) one subject does two things and (2) nothing in the sentence is parenthetical.[30]

14.4 S and S V: Two Subjects and One Verb

> Sticks and stones may break your bones.
>
> The CEO and the Chairman of the Board agree that the stock should be split.
>
> Your proposal and supporting documents are due on the tenth.
>
> Men and women have different biological imperatives.
>
> CIA and FBI have repeatedly argued about jurisdiction in this case.

Note that there is *no punctuation* when (1) two subjects take the same verb and (2) nothing is parenthetical.

14.5 IC IC: Two Independent Clauses Without Any Connecting Words

There are five different ways to punctuate between two sentences when we don't connect those sentences with words. We can use a period, a semicolon, a colon, a dash, or parentheses. The different marks direct the reader to react in different ways; they supply signals about how we intend our thoughts to relate and the varying degrees of emphasis each thought should have. What each mark suggests is explained next.

14.5.1 Use a period when you want to heavily emphasize each thought.

Thank you for writing. We appreciate hearing from our customers.

The matter requires your immediate attention. We urge you to contact us as soon as you can.

14.5.2 Use a semicolon between independent clauses when you decide that neither one deserves sentence weight.

The semicolon is a good mark to use when both structures are short and parallel:

EMC's stock rose yesterday; Nokia's stock fell.

The CFO promptly resigned; the CEO vowed to fight the accusation.

But you can use it between any two independent clauses when the clauses are relatively short and you want to suggest that the thoughts are closely related:

Thank you for writing; we appreciate hearing from our customers.

These equations are overly complex; they should be reduced to their simplest form.

14.5.3 Use a colon when the second independent clause answers the question raised by the first.

This construction, known as a "summary statement," is a particularly powerful aid to coherence.

This should teach us an important lesson: no one can afford to become complacent.

The speaker said something I thought was memorable: gravity has no sense of humor.

14.5.4 Use a dash, instead of a colon, when (1) the second independent clause amplifies the first and (2) you wish to suggest that the outcome is fairly dramatic.

The experiment suggests something incredible—the speed of light can be surpassed.

The project manager came right to the point—the overruns must stop.

14.5.5 Use parentheses around the second independent clause when you wish to indicate that the second thought is less important than the first.

We received your proposal yesterday. (The committee will evaluate it next week.)

We received your proposal yesterday (the committee will evaluate it next week).

In the examples immediately above, the period goes inside parentheses when the sentence begins in parentheses. The period goes outside parentheses when both of the independent clauses are contained in a single sentence structure. Both constructions are correct. The first maximizes the weight of *We received your proposal yesterday*. The second example dilutes emphasis on that idea because both independent clauses are contained in a single sentence structure.

> **Don't put a comma between two independent clauses when you don't supply a connecting word or phrase.**
> This is a common error, and what results is called a "comma splice" or a "run-on sentence." Below are some examples with reasonable revisions. Remember that you can use a period, a semicolon, a colon, a dash, or parentheses. The precise mark you use depends on your intended emphasis.

error: The method has one advantage, it is inexpensive.

correct: The method has one advantage: it is inexpensive.

error: We are responsible for the design, they are responsible for the construction.

correct: We are responsible for the design; they are responsible for the construction.

error: Phase One is finished, we should proceed to Phase Two.

correct: Phase One is finished. We should proceed to Phase Two.

14.6 IC, IC, and IC: A List of Three or More Short Independent Clauses

Commas suffice to separate a list of relatively simple independent clauses. Below, note how commas separate the three clauses in exactly the way they separate a list of nouns like *Sweden, Finland, and Norway*.

Sixteen exploratory wells have been drilled in Parcel 48, nine will soon be drilled in Parcel 53, and two are planned in Parcel 57.

Mr. Smith claims that his wife was driving, Mrs. Smith insists that her husband was, and neither one is willing to admit responsibility.

In these examples, semicolons are unnecessary because commas suffice to separate the ideas. For the same reason that we swat a fly with a flyswatter (and not drop a hydrogen bomb on it), we use minimal force when punctuating. Commas speed the reader along.

14.7 IC; IC; IC: A List of Three Fairly Complex Independent Clauses

In the examples below, the rules of English would allow you to use commas (instead of semicolons) to separate the three items because neither of the first two items contains any internal punctuation. You'd simply put an *and* before the last item.

Two years ago the policy was adopted by Switzerland; last year it was adopted by Canada; this year it will become law in Mexico, India, and Turkey.

Amendment I extends the deadline for the completion of Phase 3;
Amendment II increases funding by $150,000 for indirect costs;
Amendment III imposes penalties for unauthorized overtime.

So why use semicolons? Here is where you have to use judgment. Remember Principle 9: punctuation slows the reading. Semicolons provide more "stopping power" than commas. Here, you would use them instead of commas if you wish to isolate the items a little more distinctly. Doing so would emphasize each one a little more. You increase emphasis further when you present each as a separate sentence, and you maximize emphasis when you format with bullets.

14.8 IC, and IC: Two Independent Clauses Connected by Any of Eight Coordinating Conjunctions

The familiar "compound sentence" consists of two independent clauses with one of eight one-syllable words between them. These are coordinating conjunctions:

and   but   or   so   yet   nor   for   as

When you connect independent clauses with any of these words, it's conventional to *put a comma before the conjunction*.

The audit team found several discrepancies, and the bank has agreed to rectify them.

They lack experience in the field, but they bid on the contract anyway.

You can continue thinking that, or you can wake up and open your eyes.

We are going to miss our revenue numbers, so we had better prepare a press release.

The witness has been granted immunity, yet she refuses to testify.

The company did not appeal the decision within the stated time frame, nor did it request more time to file an appeal.

The corporation missed out on enormous profits, for it underestimated the demand.

The CEO resigned, as his reputation was ruined.[31]

Guidebooks on punctuation say that you have to put a comma—nothing else—in this position, but remember how effective a dash can be here:

The board of directors was certain the proposal would be accepted—and they were amazed when the shareholders rejected it.

The recommendations in this report may be brilliant—but we can't be sure because the writing is impossible to understand.

Parentheses can be effective here too:

The architects insist that the design is feasible (and they point out that it costs less than the others).

The humor consultant charges $10,000 a day (so it's clear he has a strange sense of humor).

14.9 IC; however, IC: Two Independent Clauses Connected by a Conjunctive Adverb

You don't become a better person by knowing what conjunctive adverbs are, but you become a better writer when you recognize them and have a good sense of how to handle them. They're essentially transitions: we use them to bridge from one independent clause to another, and to show readers how the second thought relates to the first. But they are not coordinating conjunctions (*and, but, or, so, yet, nor, for, as*), and they are punctuated differently.

Here are the most common conjunctive adverbs:

again	likewise
also	meanwhile

anyway	moreover
besides	nevertheless
certainly	next
consequently	nonetheless
currently	now
furthermore	otherwise
hence	similarly
however	still
incidentally	subsequently
indeed	then
instead	therefore
later	thus

When you use one of these words to link two sentences, put a comma after it:

> The prosecution presented a persuasive case. However, no one knows what the jury will decide.

> We must simplify the user manual. Otherwise, we will be flooded with calls asking for clarification.

> The discovery forces us to reexamine the most basic principles of physics. Indeed, all of our assumptions are now up for grabs.

14.9.1 Before a conjunctive adverb, use a period, a dash, a semicolon, or opening parentheses.

Let's start by understanding what our options are. When we use a conjunctive adverb, we have four choices in how to punctuate. Below, instead of the short coordinating conjunctions *and, or, yet,* and *so,* I've used their longer relatives—the conjunctive adverbs *furthermore, oth-*

erwise, nevertheless, and *therefore*—with the four conventional patterns of punctuation.

period	The advertising misleads customers about the benefits of the medication. Furthermore, it recommends using the medication for purposes the FDA has explicitly prohibited.
dash	We must act now to recall the product—otherwise, costly lawsuits are inevitable.
parentheses	Early analyses of the photographs reveal no signs of life on the planet. (Nevertheless, scientists remain hopeful that microbial life will be found.)
semicolon	The search of the suspect's guest house was illegal; therefore, all evidence proceeding from that search is inadmissible.

14.9.2 Recognize how the different marks not only suggest different logical relationships, but also indicate how you want things emphasized.

While all of the patterns indicated above are correct, one of them will provide the best "fit" in a particular construction. It's important to choose with care, because each mark suggests a different nuance of emphasis. Here's how to think about them.

If the thoughts are equally important and you want to emphasize each one, use a period. Make them separate sentences.	Dozens of onlookers insisted that a UFO had hovered over their roofs. However, what they had observed was a misbehaving Army drone.
If you wish to suggest that the second independent clause is especially dramatic or significant, use a dash.	I agree that the state has a strong case against my client—however, you may be surprised at the evidence that comes out in the trial.

If you wish to suggest that the second independent clause is less important than the first, use parentheses.	The discovery has received a lot of hype in the press (however, leading physicists remain skeptical about its importance).
If the thoughts are equally important but neither one deserves sentence weight, use a semicolon.	We submitted a proposal for the project; however, because of new commitments, we are withdrawing our bid.

It's important to remember Principle 1: you've put your thoughts in a certain order for a reason, and punctuation's job is to put a "final polish"—definitive signals about meaning and emphasis—on any sentence you write. Now we'll go through the four patterns one at a time, exploring them in more detail and looking at additional examples.

14.9.3 IC. Therefore, IC.: The Conjunctive Adverb with a Period

The two expressions below don't differ much in meaning. But they differ tremendously in emphasis and in tone.

> Plaintiff's argument lacks legal foundation, and it is frivolous and a waste of the court's time.

> Plaintiff's argument lacks legal foundation. Moreover, it is frivolous and a waste of the court's time.

As a reader, you should sense that the second expression has much more force than the first. Its strength results from two changes. First, the writer has broken the structure into two separate sentences. Each thought now stands alone, and each receives sentence weight. Second, we have elevated the word choice from *and* to *moreover*, a word whose associations with logical argument lend a more serious tone to the expression. Exactly the same principles apply to the example below.

> The company did its best to comply with the law as it understood the law, so it should not be penalized.

The company did its best to comply with the law as it understood the law. Therefore, it should not be penalized.

14.9.4 IC—nevertheless, IC.: The Conjunctive Adverb with a Dash

The dash alerts your reader that the following thought is in some way dramatic, ironic, or surprising. The mark is particularly useful in reinforcing that the second thought contrasts with the first.

The group could have given up—instead, they doubled their efforts.

The bank was informed about the money-laundering activities of the cartel—nonetheless, it continued doing business with the group.

The State Department swore it would never negotiate with terrorists—meanwhile, it was secretly bargaining for the hostages' release.

14.9.5 IC (incidentally, IC).: The Conjunctive Adverb with Parentheses

The Federal Trade Commission has voiced concerns about a monopoly (still, the merger will probably proceed).

Dr. Maia Callabar will be the featured speaker. (Incidentally, she used to work for this company.)

Our attorneys are baffled by the complaint, but they say they can get it dismissed. (Anyway, no judge in his right mind would hear the case.)

Parentheses tell your reader to regard the second thought as being relatively minor in importance—that it's the kind of thought you would preface, in speaking, with "by the way." You can't expect your reader to get this sense if you don't use parentheses for the purpose.

14.9.6 IC; besides, IC.: The Conjunctive Adverb with a Semicolon

We have some reservations about her experience; besides, she has clearly stated that she would be unable to relocate until early next year.

> The contract stipulates that Task B must be completed by June 30; however, it does not state what penalties (if any) would be imposed if this deadline is not met.

Most writers are comfortable with the semicolon here. The problem is, they're so comfortable with it that they use it in such constructions all the time, even when a different mark would better suggest their intention. When you use a semicolon to connect two sentences, all you are doing is reducing emphasis on the thoughts. Sometimes, yes, that's what you want to do. But you should consider the other three options first.

Keep in mind that every time you use a semicolon in front of a conjunctive adverb, you could use a period instead. Especially when your clauses are lengthy, using a period makes much more sense.

14.10 IC. For example, IC.: Two Independent Clauses Connected by a Transitional Phrase

You punctuate these in exactly the same way you punctuate one-word conjunctive adverbs. Here are examples of the four possible patterns:

period	The airline spokesman said that the plane "experienced an unintended impact with the ground." In other words, it crashed.
dash	A recession is not imminent—on the contrary, most important indicators point to accelerating growth in GDP this year.
parentheses	The company's president, in his typical quirky manner, told reporters that his small corporation is "overcowed by the lust of the marketplace" (that is, the company can't produce enough cursing alarm clocks to meet the unexpected demand).
semicolon	Most of our customers find nothing difficult about the controls; in fact, many have written to say they have found the device surprisingly easy to use.

Some common transitional phrases:

as a result	in other words
by comparison	in particular
for example	in the interim
in consequence	on the contrary
in contrast	on the other hand
in fact	that is

Precisely the same thinking that applies to punctuating conjunctive adverbs applies to these phrases. Use the mark that best suggests your intent. Don't use a semicolon just because it's correct, or because you used a dash in a document yesterday, or because your freshman composition instructor had a morbid dread of parentheses and insisted that they were incorrect, too casual, too informal, signs of laziness, evidence of flimsy thinking, footprints of a bonehead, or proof of the devil.

Never forget this: Your reader reads what you write. She cannot read your mind. Your job as a writer is to get your intention expressed in your structures of language. Your intention consists not only of meaning, but also of emphasis—and as the writer, you're responsible for encoding both.

Appendix: How to List Ideas

The list is as old as writing itself. The Ten Commandments is a list. The Code of Hammurabi (the first code of law, written about 4,000 years ago) is a breathtakingly plain list of hundreds of offenses and the punishments for committing them. Each time you jot "milk, eggs, Advil" on a scrap of paper before leaving the house, you are behaving like an ancient sage. The list is a primeval device, born from two hardheaded desires: to avoid unnecessary repetition and to reinforce the sense that items belong together. It has survived because of these twin efficiencies.

Lists Take Three Shapes

They can maintain the appearance of a sentence; they can maintain the appearance of a paragraph; and they can be formatted vertically, with bullets, numbers, or letters. The first two shapes do not jump out when the reader glances at the page. The vertical list does. Whether the vertical format is appropriate in a short (two- or three-item) list therefore depends on whether you wish to heavily emphasize the items. It is usually the best choice when your list is lengthy.

Maintaining the Shape of the Sentence

Only a comma is required for clarity when you list single words or short phrases. In the following examples, note that the serial (final) comma is included.

verbs	We have to decide whether to accept, reject, or renegotiate the contract.
nouns	Chaucer's tales are bursting with comical nuns, monks, and friars.
adverbs	The repairs were completed quickly, thoroughly, and efficiently.
adjectives	His resignation speech was surly, brutish, and abrupt.
short phrases	We will fight them on the beaches, in the fields, and in the streets.

If some of the items in the list require internal punctuation, the comma alone won't clearly separate the ideas. If only one of the items has internal punctuation, use parentheses around the modifying phrase. In the example below, *which is especially important to the region* does not have the same status as an item in the list.

unduly difficult:	They examined photographs of the Red Sea, the Strait of Hormuz, which is especially important to the region, and the Persian Gulf.
instantly clear:	They examined photographs of the Red Sea, the Strait of Hormuz (which is especially important to the region), and the Persian Gulf.

If more than one of the items have internal punctuation, separate them either with semicolons or with numbers in parentheses. Numbers work better than semicolons when the items are relatively lengthy or complex. If you number each item, the comma suffices to separate them.

Subpoenas were issued for Stancil Reese, CFO of Erolutions, Inc; Anastasia D'Ambrosio, CFO of Tapcom; and Corbin Quiles, COO of Vestek.

> The purpose of this correspondence is (1) to provide you with a signed modification that makes incremental funds available to your contract, (2) to request a revised budget proposal to cover the period November 2008 through March 2013, and (3) to remind you that your annual summary report is now overdue.

The use of *(i), (ii), (iii), (iv),* and so on is most often seen in legal writing, where it is traditional. It achieves the same purpose, but let's acknowledge that *(1), (2),* and *(3)* are simpler. Let's also agree that nothing good can come from a desire to make our style look "legal." Leave the little Roman numerals to lawyers.

We sometimes see *(a), (b),* and *(c)* used instead of numerals. The letters serve the same purpose, but because they must be used when citing particular sections of law, rule, and policy, it's best not to use them merely to separate items in a list.

No rule requires that you use parentheses on both sides of the number, but readability research consistently indicates that readers stumble over *1), 2),* and *3).* It's best to use parentheses on both sides. In no case should you include a period—never write *(1.), (a.), (i.), 1.),* etc., in the middle of a sentence.

Maintaining the Shape of the Paragraph

Ordinary paragraphs, regardless of how coherent they are, disguise lists. I think it's perfectly reasonable to argue that the paragraph below contains a list of ideas. In this case, the three ideas in the list are separate sentences, each of which supports the topic sentence, and the writer does a good job of showing how the thoughts relate with *First, Second,* and *Third.*

> The implications are vivid. First, our major competitors are spending more than we do on advertising and, as a direct result, they are capturing more of the market. Second, they are rapidly increasing their advertising outlay, which will clearly result in their further outdistancing us in terms of revenue and market share. Third, by investing more in advertising, we can enhance our revenue and our competitive position.

Don't get me wrong—that's a well-written paragraph. The fact remains that if you want the reader to see the three supporting sentences as a list, you make your intention plain when you write it this way:

> The implications are vivid. (1) Our major competitors are spending more than we do on advertising and, as a direct result, they are capturing more of the market. (2) They are rapidly increasing their advertising outlay, which will clearly result in their further outdistancing us in terms of revenue and market share. (3) By investing more in advertising, we can enhance our revenue and our competitive position.

This paragraph would be improved if the lead-in sentence did a better job of framing the list for the reader. "Framing" means that you *characterize* what follows; this enables the reader to regard the ideas in the way you intend. The example below frames the list as *three important conclusions.*

> We can draw three important conclusions from the study. (1) Our major competitors are spending more than we do on advertising and, as a direct result, they are capturing more of the market. (2) They are rapidly increasing their advertising outlay, which will clearly result in their further outdistancing us in terms of revenue and market share. (3) By investing more in advertising, we can enhance our revenue and our competitive position.

But what's important here is that the list retains its shape *as a paragraph.* Certainly, the writer could gush the entire thing as a single sentence, with a colon after the lead-in and semicolons after the first two items. But that would annihilate emphasis because it would minimize separation of the items. It would not be a good idea, at least not if we want the reader to consider each thought. The other alternative would be to format the three supporting sentences in a vertical list—this is feasible, and we'll look at examples of it in a minute—but the vertical format is strongly emphatic. And sometimes we need a sort of middle ground between the mild emphasis supplied by *First, Second, Third*, on the one hand, and the attention-grabbing vertical list on the other.

When this is the case, simply write a strong topic sentence and number the sentences that support it.

The Vertical List

Readers benefit from the vertical format, and you should use it whenever your list is relatively lengthy or the items are complex. You should also use it, even in a short list, when you wish to strongly emphasize the items. The format differs visually from that of ordinary sentences and paragraphs, and thus it attracts the reader's attention. It doesn't do that if you overuse it, so be judicious; using too many vertical lists results in a document that looks like an outline.

Vertical lists come in two forms. The more common is the one that breaks up a sentence. The second is the one that breaks up a paragraph.

Breaking Up a Single Sentence

List ideas vertically when, for any reason, the vertical format best serves clarity or emphasis. There is no rule governing how many items your list must have in order for a vertical format to be appropriate. Sometimes, in fact, only a pair of items is best presented in bullets. This is especially true when each item is complicated. Even for experts in the slippery concepts of accounting, the expression below poses grave problems.

> Cash flows from commitments accounted for as derivatives under SFAS No. 133, "Accounting for Derivative Instruments and Hedging Activities," that result in the acquisition or sale of mortgage securities or mortgage loans are classified as either investing activities for available-for-sale securities or mortgage loans classified as held-for-investment or operating activities for trading securities or mortgage loans classified as held-for-sale.

When we break it up, the intended readers have a much easier time understanding it.

> When a commitment is considered a derivative under SFAS No. 133 ("Accounting for Derivative Instruments and Hedging Activities") and its cash flow is affected by the acquisition or sale of mortgage securities or mortgage loans, that cash flow must be classified in one of two ways:
>
> - as *investing activities* for available-for-sale securities or for mortgage loans classified as held-for-investment
>
> - as *operating activities* for trading securities or for mortgage loans classified as held-for-sale

Yes, I have changed the order of the words to clarify the meaning, and I have italicized two key terms to present them in clear light. Format alone is never sufficient. My point is that bullets are sometimes useful even for *two* ideas.

Now we're going to look at three examples of vertical lists that separate the elements of a single sentence.

EXAMPLE 1—BREAKING UP A SENTENCE

Original:

> To assist us in the planning process, please let me know your availability to attend, your interest in participating as a speaker, panelist, or poster presenter, and any topics or themes you would like to suggest.[1]

Revision 1:

> To assist us in planning the event, please let me know
>
> - your availability to attend
>
> - your interest in participating as a speaker, panelist, or poster presenter
>
> - any topics or themes you would like to suggest

Revision 2:

> To assist us in planning the event, please let me know the following:
>
> - your availability to attend

- your interest in participating as a speaker, panelist, or poster presenter

- any topics or themes you would like to suggest

Both revisions are fine. The only difference between Revision 1 and Revision 2 is how the lead-in expression is structured. In Revision 1, the lead-in is an incomplete thought, and no punctuation follows it. (Put a colon there if you believe you must or if your manager demands it. The reader does not need it.) In Revision 2, the lead-in is a complete thought, and convention requires that it be followed by a colon.

Note that no punctuation at all follows the bulleted items. When you use bullets to break up a single sentence, your list comprises fragments of that sentence. Listed vertically, fragments are not punctuated. There are no commas or semicolons after the items, and there is no period at the end. Format has taken the place of what punctuation would otherwise have to accomplish—it shows the reader how the items are separated and indicates where the list ends. When we use vertical format, we are no longer writing a sentence, and the ordinary rules of punctuation no longer apply.

I had better mention that in everyday business writing, people sprinkle punctuation onto such lists with the zeal of novice chefs sprinkling too much pepper on a casserole. Yes, you often see a comma or a semicolon after each item, an *and* after the next-to-last item, and a period at the end. But readers do not need those signals. And when we remember that readers have to process every keystroke on the page, it becomes clear that we should not punctuate when the marks accomplish nothing.

EXAMPLE 2—BREAKING UP A SENTENCE

In the next example, the original sentence disregards the limits of human comprehension. Compassion for the reader is always in order. The writer of the sentence apparently forgot something called the Golden Rule. If as a reader he would not want to read it or would struggle to understand it, then as a writer he should not create it.

Original:

"Sexual harassment" is defined as sexual advances, requests for sexual favors, and verbal or physical conduct of a sexual nature when submission to or rejection of such advances, requests, or conduct is made either explicitly or implicitly a condition of employment or a basis for continuing employment and such advances, requests, or conduct have the purpose or effect of unreasonably interfering with an individual's work performance by creating an intimidating, hostile, humiliating, or sexually offensive work environment.[2]

Revision:

"Sexual harassment" is defined as sexual advances, requests for sexual favors, and verbal or physical conduct of a sexual nature when either of the following is true:

- your submitting to or rejecting such advances, requests, or conduct is made (explicitly or implicitly) a condition of employment, or a basis for continuing employment

- such advances, requests, or conduct have the purpose or effect of unreasonably interfering with your work performance by creating an intimidating, hostile, humiliating, or sexually offensive work environment

EXAMPLE 3—BREAKING UP A SENTENCE

In this example, the writer uses semicolons to separate the items. As is so often the case, using semicolons results in an expression that's "correct English" but is unduly difficult to read. You cannot know, at a glance, that the sentence embodies a list, and you have to read it twice to determine exactly how many kinds of information are required.

> Since each delegation's visit is unique and requires considerable research and logistical planning, the party requesting a briefing should provide the International Visitors' Bureau with the name, professional title, organizational affiliation, mailing address, telephone number, fax number, and email address of the party requesting the briefing; the country or countries represented by the briefing; a preferred and alternate date and time for the briefing; background materials about the delegation, including the name, professional title, and biographical information or resume of each delegate; and the issues or specific questions the delegation would like to discuss, ranked in descending order of importance.

I'm going to go out on a limb and state that readers—not most readers, but *all* readers—have an easier time understanding what's required if we format the list like this:

> Since each delegation's visit is unique and requires considerable research and logistical planning, the party requesting a briefing should provide the International Visitors' Bureau with the following information:

- the name, professional title, organizational affiliation, mailing address, telephone number, fax number, and email address of the party requesting the briefing

- the country or countries represented by the briefing

- a preferred and alternate date and time for the briefing

- background materials about the delegation, including the name, professional title, and biographical information or resume of each delegate

- the issues or specific questions the delegation would like to discuss, ranked in descending order of importance

In this example, using numbers to precede each item would not be a bad idea. The writer may have listed the items from most important to least important, and in any event the reader would benefit by seeing that she needs to provide five bits of information.

Since each delegation's visit is unique and requires considerable research and logistical planning, the party requesting a briefing should provide the International Visitors' Bureau with the following information:

1. the name, professional title, organizational affiliation, mailing address, telephone number, fax number, and email address of the party requesting the briefing

2. the country or countries represented by the briefing

3. a preferred and alternate date and time for the briefing

4. background materials about the delegation, including the name, professional title, and biographical information or resume of each delegate

5. the issues or specific questions the delegation would like to discuss, ranked in descending order of importance

Breaking Up a Paragraph

When you break a paragraph into a vertical list, each bulleted item is a sentence and is treated accordingly. It begins with a capital letter, is punctuated as necessary, and ends with a period. The topic sentence, which serves as a lead-in, ends with a period, not with a colon.

EXAMPLE 1—BREAKING UP A PARAGRAPH

I used this example earlier to show how we can maintain the shape of the paragraph by preceding each sentence with a number. This time I'll format it vertically.

We can draw three important conclusions from the study. First, our major competitors are spending more than we do on advertising and, as a direct result, they are capturing more of the market. Second, our competitors are rapidly increasing their advertising outlay, which will clearly result in their further outdistancing us in terms of revenue and market share. Third, by investing more in advertising, we can enhance our revenue and our competitive position.

In the revision, note (1) the period after the lead-in sentence, (2) the capitalized first word of each bulleted item, and (3) the period at the end of each item.

> We can draw three important conclusions from the study.

- Our major competitors are spending more than we do on advertising and, as a direct result, they are capturing more of the market.

- Our competitors are rapidly increasing their advertising outlay, which will clearly result in their further outdistancing us in terms of revenue and market share.

- By investing more in advertising, we can enhance our revenue and our competitive position.

You could use numbers instead of bullets:

> We can draw three important conclusions from the study.

1. Our major competitors are spending more than we do on advertising and, as a direct result, they are capturing more of the market.

2. Our competitors are rapidly increasing their advertising outlay, which will clearly result in their further outdistancing us in terms of revenue and market share.

3. By investing more in advertising, we can enhance our revenue and our competitive position.

But using numbers here would not be a good idea, and for two reasons. First, the reader is told at the outset (and can instantly see) that the list comprises three things; he does not need to be further informed of it. Second, numbers would suggest that you have ranked the conclusions from most important to least important, and in this expression that does not seem to be the case. In this expression, the three conclusions appear equally important.

EXAMPLE 2—BREAKING UP A PARAGRAPH

In the paragraph below, each sentence is well written. The writer does a nice job of engaging the reader by phrasing the items of the list as questions.

> When choosing a wireless phone plan, you should ask yourself a number of questions. Where, how, and when will you use your cell phone? Will most of your calls be made in your local area, or will you call all around the nation? When will you use your cell phone the most—in the daytime, or during evenings and weekends? Will you use your cell phone only in case of emergencies? How much are you willing to spend on wireless service each month?

We can make the questions more accessible by using the vertical format, and we make them more engaging by phrasing them from the reader's point of view (in other words, by using *I* and *my* instead of *you* and *your*).

> Before choosing a wireless phone plan, ask yourself these questions.

- Where, how, and when will I use my cell phone?

- Will I make most calls in my local area, or will I call all around the nation?

- When will I use my cell phone the most—in the daytime, or during evenings and weekends?

- Will I use my cell phone only in case of emergencies?

- How much am I willing to spend on wireless service each month?

Should I Use Bullets, Numbers, or Letters in a Vertical List?

Bullets are best when you don't wish to imply that the items are listed either by priority or by required sequence. Use bullets when the items are equally important.

Numbers suggest ranking in importance. They are also more informative than bullets when your list consists of a series of sequential steps.

Lowercase letters are necessary to indicate ranking or sequence in any kind of document where every paragraph is already numbered for reference. This is true of most legal and regulatory writing, and is often the convention in quasi-legal documents such as proposals and policies. Otherwise, you really don't need to use letters unless you have a multi-level list, where there are sub-ideas or sub-steps under an already bulleted item. Using letters is not wrong, and in some professions and organizations their use is standard.

Be consistent. You must be consistent in the symbol you use to preface the items in lists throughout the document. If you shift from bullets to asterisks, for example, readers may wonder what distinction you are trying to draw. Shift only when you have reason to shift. For example, shift from bullets to numbers when items in the first list are of equal importance but the items in the second list must be performed sequentially.

Avoid dingbats. Other symbols are occasionally used before each item in a vertical list. It's not rare to see the asterisk and the hyphen used instead of bullets. These do the job perfectly well. But rightward-pointing fingers, shooting stars, bombs, flowers, and so forth are whimsical and are best limited to corkboard announcements of the company picnic or schedule of the softball team.

Notes

Introduction

1. http://www.iolani.honolulu.hi.us/Keables/KeablesGuide/Part Four/TitlesEndPunctDashesParen.htm

2. http://jeremy.zawodny.com/blog/archives/000296.html

3. http://lists.musicbrainz.org/pipermail/musicbrainz-style/2006 November/004163.html

Author's Note

1. Some professionals in fields such as academia and book publishing are wedded to particular style guides whose principles vary somewhat from those found here. They're entitled to their preferences.

What You Need to Know First: 19 Principles

1. Principle 13 explains this issue in detail.

2. You often have alternative ways to punctuate. The different sorts of emphasis supplied by various marks—and why the marks influence the reader as they do—are covered in detail in Principle 8.

3. I should have said "made less puzzling," because the expression remains difficult. The fault here is word choice. *Used* is a bad choice, since what most people do with candy is *eat* it. What the wrapper should say is simply *Best when eaten before December 10, 2009.*

4. The serial comma is the comma that goes after the next-to-last item in your list (right before *and* or *or*) when you list things in a sentence. I discuss this particular comma in detail in Principle 14.

5. In workplace writing, this issue—knowing how to indicate whether an expression is restrictive or non-restrictive—is the most common source of error in punctuation. Because it's important, I address it in detail in Principle 11.

6. When we write, we isolate ideas in numerous ways. For example, we use boldface or italics to distinguish a particularly important sentence or phrase; we skip a line between a heading and the text it governs; we write a single-sentence paragraph; we use larger type size for a title, then center it and surround it with white space, to make sure it stands out; we put a period after a short independent clause when we want the thought to have punch.

7. Notice that in the better alternatives, the subject and the verb are side by side. This is what I mean by "straightforward." In the writing we do at work, it's the right pattern to follow.

8. Don't be intimidated by the term "subordinate." All it means is that you use a simple trick of grammar to show the reader that one thought is less significant than another.

9. Here I am discussing the matter of whether we use any punctuation at all. The other confusing sense of "optional" refers to situations where you have a choice of several different marks (commas, dashes, or parentheses, for example). That issue is discussed in Principles 7 and 8.

10. You may know this particular comma as the "Harvard comma" or the "Oxford comma." Like any good English-teacher term, it has to have at least two aliases.

11. Even though most newspapers routinely omit the serial comma, they grudgingly pop it in when absolutely necessary to prevent misunderstanding. Here are two consecutive sentences from an article in the *Washington Post* (note how the serial comma is included in the first sentence but omitted from the second): *The Pentagon has outlined three basic options: send in more troops, shrink the force but stay longer, or pull out. Insiders have dubbed these three views "Go Long," "Go Short" and "Go Home."*

12. Assuming that Samuel Beckett and God are not the writer's parents, the serial comma should appear after *Beckett*. Assuming that the writer does not intend to characterize the former British Prime Minister as a 60-year-old virgin who collects dildos, the serial comma should appear after *virgin*. A nearly identical sentence appeared in the *London Times*.

13. A surprising number of people will go to their graves insisting that, without exception, *a* precedes a consonant and *an* precedes a vowel. This is what they were taught, and despite thousands of examples of evidence to the contrary, it is what they believe, because it is what they were taught. They will think you have made an error if you write *an FCC policy* or *a European office*.

The Marks

1. Hundreds of years ago, there was no *her* in English. *His* was used for both genders. Thus, people would talk about *the blacksmith his shop* (and contract it to *the blacksmith's shop*) and *the lady his ring* (contracting it to *the lady's ring*). That's why, to this day, we use *'s* to show ownership.

2. The device *sic* is explained in 2.4.

3. *Sic* can also follow archaic usage. Quoting from the U.S. Constitution, "The House of Representatives shall chuse their Speaker . . . ." *Chuse* was the correct spelling when the Constitution was written, but you don't want your reader to think you've misspelled it when quoting. For certain audiences it's a good idea to write, "The House of Representatives shall chuse [*sic*] their Speaker . . . ."

4. There is no agreement on whether the first letter of the summary statement should be capitalized. Just be consistent.

5. The colon here, after *in*, is an error in usage because it accomplishes nothing. It is always an error to put a colon after a preposition, simply because your intended meaning never requires it.

6. Lists take many forms, and it's important that you choose the most efficient "shape" for any list of ideas. There are several distinct types of vertical lists; each requires different punctuation. For a complete explanation of how to handle the matter, please see the appendix, "How to List Ideas."

7. When you use a ratio as an adjective—when you put it before a noun—use hyphens instead of a colon. The ratio is 10:1, but it is a *10-to-1 ratio* and a *50-to-1 chance*.

8. In typeset material, there is usually only one space after the colon and after the punctuation mark at the end of a sentence. This book is an example of that style. But keep in mind that the compositor—the individual who actually arranges every symbol on a printed page—has at his disposal a number of devices for subtly adjusting space and keeping things readable. You and I have only a keyboard. The recently amended *Publication Manual of the American Psychological Association*, commonly known as the *APA Manual*, now recommends spacing twice after the punctuation mark at the end of a sentence for any text that is not typeset. That's sensible guidance, and I hope you follow it, especially since the stuff we write at work isn't typeset.

9. This particular usage gives many writers fits. If you're unsure about the distinction between coordinate and cumulative adjectives, refer to Principle 15.

10. I know there's a lot of debate about this particular comma. Much of the debate is wrongheaded and overgeneralized. The bottom line is that clarity is never harmed when you insert this comma, but it's often harmed when you don't. Readers who skip around are encouraged to refer to Principle 14.

11. See 12.5–12.7 for a discussion of how semicolons, numbers, and bullets can be helpful in this regard.

12. For a fuller explanation and additional examples, see 14.2 and Principle 13.

13. Beware. Carelessly handled, such constructions lead to the most common error in syntax—the famous "dangling modifier," where the writer puts the wrong word after the opening phrase. *Howling at the moon, I thought the wolves epitomized the wilderness* is an example. Only if *you* were howling at the moon does that sentence embody your intention.

14. Commas are required in these examples, and required to be where they are, because of rules mentioned earlier. In the first example, we have a dependent clause followed by an independent clause (see 4.11). In the second, the commas come where they would come in *apples, bananas, and oranges* (see 4.8). In the third, we have two independent clauses connected with *but* (see 4.9).

15. You may encounter occasions when a dash fits before the other coordinating conjunctions (*so, or,* and *yet*). These occasions will be far less frequent than those involving *and* and *but*, which is why I've used those two words in the examples.

16. The other (and simpler) way to express this idea is *He served as Director from 2005 to 2010.*

17. Principle 16 discusses improvised usage in detail.

18. Examples of comparative adjectives are *bigger, brighter, stranger.* Examples of superlatives are *biggest, brightest, strangest.* Just a reminder.

19. Here the parentheses enclose what amounts to a "translation" of a term. Common sense argues that you'd do the same thing with unfamiliar foreign words and phrases. *The name of the Russian space station is* Mir *("peace"). She works for the Bundesbank (the German central bank, equivalent to the Federal Reserve Bank).*

20. *Maker(s)* is unnecessary because the word *I* refers to anyone who signs the note. If two or more people sign, *I* refers to them all. The phrase *recognize(s) and acknowledge*(s) is an ancient, ill-conceived legal term of art that means *agree.*

21. Here, instead of the semicolon, you could use a period. Doing so would increase emphasis on both thoughts.

22. Federal government employees usually follow the guidance in the *GPO Style Manual.* Others can benefit from the *Associated Press Stylebook* or the *Chicago Manual of Style. The MLA Handbook for Writers of Research Papers* (usually called "the MLA") is possibly more useful in academic writing than in business, regulatory, and technical writing. Many private-sector organizations follow the guidance of the *Publication Manual of the American Psychological Association*, commonly known as the *APA Manual.*

23. The plural form of *Mr.* is *Messrs*; the plural of *Dr.* is *Drs.*; the plural of *Mrs.* is *Mmes.*

24. The abbreviation *n.b.* is Latin for *nota bene* ("note well"), and *z.B.* is the German abbreviation for *zum Beispiel* ("for example"). If an abbreviation is unfamiliar to your reader, does it matter what foreign language it comes from?

25. In business, technical, scientific, and regulatory writing, exclamation points are rare. It's best to confine the use of this mark to relaxed occasions (e.g., announcing a corporate picnic, announcing that a co-worker has just given birth, drumming up support for donations to a charity, and so forth).

26. But *The information, according to McLaren, "does not fully explain the situation."* Here the comma precedes the fragment because *according to McLaren* is parenthetical and must be punctuated.

27. Keep in mind that these examples come from newspaper journalism, where using bullets is not an option. In workplace writing, a vertical list would make the ideas much more accessible.

28. This is from a Presolicitation Notice issued by a federal agency. It represents only the second half of a paragraph twice its length. I'd like to add that this is not the worst example of semicolon infestation I've seen.

29. I'm not making this up. The U.S. Patent Office receives thousands of applications seeking patents for such things as lip clips, dog bumpers, and baby-bottom art. For an interesting selection of peculiar inventions, visit http://totallyabsurd.com/archive.htm.

30. There are occasional exceptions, but these happen when a writer isn't careful enough with phrasing. Remember *They ate and then robbed the manager.*

31. In the last two examples, *for* and *as* have the meaning of *because.* If you use *because* in these examples, no punctuation is necessary. If you use *for* or *as*, a comma is necessary to prevent an initial misreading, as in *We were unprepared as we expected a different outcome.* You should keep in mind that using *for* for *because* is outmoded and strikes many readers as awkward or effete.

A note to grammar purists. I realize that the *as* in this example might be termed a subordinating conjunction. Does that make any difference? The practical writer doesn't care about the academic classification of words. He simply wants to know how to handle them.

Appendix: How to List Ideas

1. This is from correspondence. One of the institutes of NIH is inviting a researcher to participate in a conference.

2. This is boilerplate language used by countless organizations and government agencies to define sexual harassment. It has been approved by attorneys, but it's ethically irresponsible to readers.

Index